MYTHBUSTING FOR TRAINEE TEACHERS

Sara Miller McCune founded SAGE Publishing in 1965 to support the dissemination of usable knowledge and educate a global community. SAGE publishes more than 1000 journals and over 800 new books each year, spanning a wide range of subject areas. Our growing selection of library products includes archives, data, case studies and video. SAGE remains majority owned by our founder and after her lifetime will become owned by a charitable trust that secures the company's continued independence.

Los Angeles | London | New Delhi | Singapore | Washington DC | Melbourne

MYTHBUSTING FOR TRAINEE TEACHERS

JONATHAN GLAZZARD
AND SAMUEL STONES

Learning Matters
A SAGE Publishing Company
1 Oliver's Yard
55 City Road
London EC1Y 1SP

SAGE Publications Inc.
2455 Teller Road
Thousand Oaks, California 91320

SAGE Publications India Pvt Ltd
B 1/I 1 Mohan Cooperative Industrial Area
Mathura Road
New Delhi 110 044

SAGE Publications Asia-Pacific Pte Ltd
3 Church Street
#10-04 Samsung Hub
Singapore 049483

Editor: Amy Thornton
Senior project editor: Chris Marke
Project management: Swales & Willis Ltd, Exeter,
Devon
Marketing manager: Lorna Patkai
Cover design: Wendy Scott
Typeset by: C&M Digitals (P) Ltd, Chennai, India
Printed in the UK

Library of Congress Control Number: 2020933770

British Library Cataloguing in Publication data

A catalogue record for this book is available from
the British Library

ISBN 978-1-5297-0987-2
ISBN 978-1-5297-0986-5 (pbk)

At SAGE we take sustainability seriously. Most of our products are printed in the UK using responsibly sourced
papers and boards. When we print overseas we ensure sustainable papers are used as measured by the
PREPS grading system. We undertake an annual audit to monitor our sustainability.

CONTENTS

ABOUT THE AUTHORS

Jonathan Glazzard is Professor of Inclusive Education at Leeds Beckett University. He is the professor attached to the Carnegie Centre of Excellence for Mental Health in Schools. Professor Glazzard teaches across a range of QTS and non-QTS programmes and is an experienced teacher educator, having previously been head of academic development at Leeds Trinity University and head of primary initial teacher training courses at the University of Huddersfield. Jonathan is a qualified teacher and taught in primary schools before moving into higher education.

Samuel Stones is a doctoral student, lecturer and researcher in the Carnegie School of Education at Leeds Beckett University. His research outputs are linked with the Centre for LGBTQ+ Inclusion in Education and the Carnegie Centre of Excellence for Mental Health in Schools. Samuel currently supervises dissertation students on a range of postgraduate courses and he works with initial teacher training students in university and school contexts. Samuel also holds a national training role for a multi-academy trust and is also an associate leader and head of year at a secondary school and sixth form college in North Yorkshire.

iNTRODUCTiON

This book introduces some key educational myths. It has been written at a time when school leaders and teachers are demonstrating greater interest in evidence-based educational practice. In a climate of financial restraints on schools, it seems logical for school leaders to invest funding into educational interventions that are based on robust research and which have been proven to work in a variety of educational contexts.

Within a climate of marketisation and school accountability, government educational policy promotes a 'what works' mindset. This has been supported by a range of organisations, including the Education Endowment Foundation (EEF) and the National Foundation for Educational Research (NFER). These organisations have invested significant funds into commissioning large-scale research projects to produce robust evidence of 'what works' within school contexts. In 2014, the EEF published the Sutton Trust toolkit (Higgins et al., 2014). This is a user-friendly resource that demonstrates the impact of a range of educational interventions. This has been used to support school leaders in making decisions about which interventions to fund. High-impact and low-cost interventions are clearly preferable to high-cost interventions that produce low-impact.

The move towards teaching as an evidence-based profession should be applauded. After all, teaching is a profession. It demands specialist subject and pedagogical knowledge and it deserves, but does not always receive, high status. Medical professionals would never prescribe medical treatments that have not been robustly tested through clinical trials. Teachers need to be assured that educational interventions have been tested and evaluated before they are adopted in the classroom. Research should inform teaching so that educational practice has strong, robust theoretical underpinning.

So, what is the problem? Children and young people are unique and so are schools. There is no guarantee that because an intervention 'works' with specific students in specific contexts, it will have the same effect on others in different contexts. Even within a school, specific interventions will 'work' with some students but not with others. Context is important.

However, there is a further danger to consider. It could be argued that the government has used the research which has been commissioned by these organisations to promote specific pedagogical approaches. These approaches are documented in various publications, including the Early Career Framework (DfE, 2019a) and the ITT Core Content Framework (DfE, 2019b), which have also been endorsed by the EEF. Many of the approaches in these documents are reductive. There is a focus on knowledge-based teaching, knowledge retrieval and memorisation. Those training to teach and early career teachers will be expected to understand more about the memory. In addition, differentiation, which was once the gold standard of effective teaching, particularly in primary education, is discouraged. There is strong emphasis on teacher-directed pedagogical approaches rather than collaborative or experiential learning. While these aspects all play an important role in the process of learning, they reduce learning to an individual rather than a social process. They reflect a behaviourist approach to learning and effectively ignore social constructivist approaches, which also play an important role in children's learning and development. Within these documents, the teacher is positioned as the expert and children are largely viewed as passive recipients of knowledge. There is an emphasis on learning and retrieving facts and developing strategies to strengthen knowledge recall.

A variety of pedagogical approaches are required to suit different purposes. Effective teachers know that they need a 'toolkit'. From this, they can select the 'tools' (pedagogical approaches) that best suit the job at hand. They will need different 'tools' to do different jobs and they will need to vary these accordingly to meet the different needs of the learners with whom they are working. One size does not fit all.

The field of educational research demonstrates a range of contradictory findings, and it is relatively straightforward to find studies that support a preferred approach. However, schools are not scientific laboratories, teachers are not technicians, and children are not robots. One of the great privileges of being a teacher is to retain the right to problem-solve your own practice. Teachers need to be trusted to use their own initiative and to make pedagogical decisions that are in the best interests of the students they teach. An off-the-shelf strategy might save teachers time, but there is no guarantee that it will work. Teachers are experts in their own practice. They are intellectuals and capable of making sound pedagogical choices. They can be guided in their practice, but they should never be told how to teach.

Within the current educational climate, it might reasonably be argued that teachers are being de-professionalised and re-professionalised. Research is being used to promote specific pedagogical approaches and these approaches are then integrated into notions of effective teaching against which teachers are evaluated. This book addresses key educational myths but also presents research that both supports and contradicts government policy.

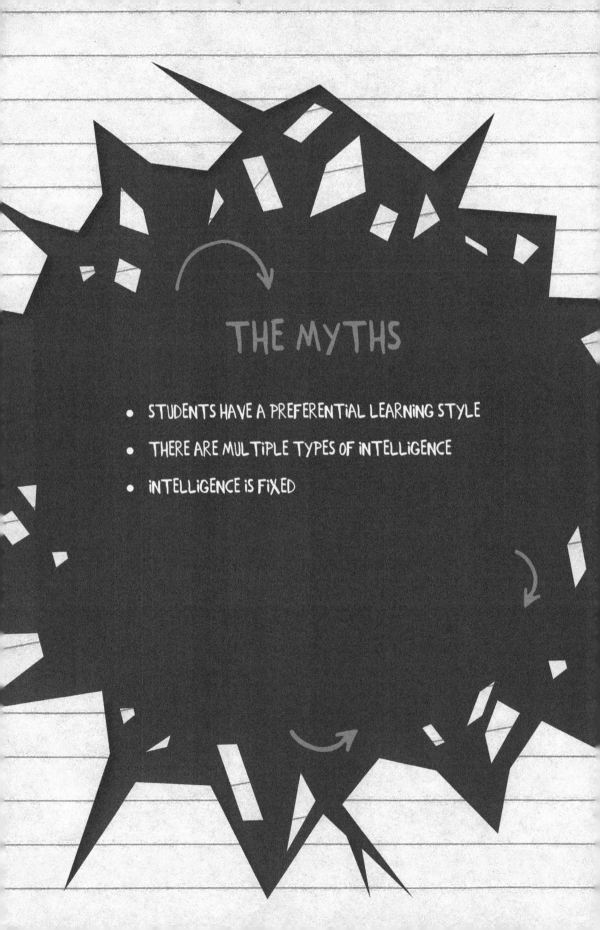

THE MYTHS

- STUDENTS HAVE A PREFERENTIAL LEARNING STYLE
- THERE ARE MULTIPLE TYPES OF INTELLIGENCE
- INTELLIGENCE IS FIXED

1
LEARNING STYLES AND INTELLIGENCE

What will you learn?

This chapter addresses common myths in relation to our understanding of learning styles and intelligence. Psychological evidence is presented to support teachers to challenge the existing research in relation to learning styles. The chapter emphasises that this evidence demonstrates there are no benefits for learners in having information presented to them through their preferred style. It also argues that the commercialisation of learning styles theory has been problematic and has created confusion among educators in relation to credibility and impact. The chapter offers a case study to illustrate some effective practice and to encourage you to reflect on your current approaches. Additionally, this chapter presents literature and research to demonstrate how our understanding of intelligence has been challenged in recent years. Through this discussion, we address common myths in relation to multiple types of intelligence and the concept of fixed intelligence. Case study material is provided to highlight the implications of these assumptions in relation to our teaching and to support your understanding of effective practice.

WHAT ARE THE MYTHS?

- Students have a preferential learning style.
- There are multiple types of intelligence.
- Intelligence is fixed.

Why should teachers challenge the myths?

The term 'learning styles' has often been adopted uncritically as part of the day-to-day vocabulary of teachers. The theory assumes that students have a dominant channel (visual, auditory or kinaesthetic) through which learning is optimised. Based on this assumption, it is assumed that if instruction is matched to the preferred style, then learning will be more effective. The theory has direct practical importance for teachers if it is accepted. Once a learning style has been assessed and identified through a learning style inventory, then teaching approaches can be adapted to enable the student to learn through their dominant style. There are several models (e.g. Honey and Mumford, 2000; Kolb, 1984), each accompanied by an assessment tool that seeks to identify a dominant style based on an individual's responses to a series of questions about their learning behaviour. Each model has its own associated technical vocabulary (Coffield et al., 2004a, 2004b) and opposing categories, known as dichotomies. However, this theory is not supported by research evidence and potentially could restrict learning opportunities.

The second assumption is that there are varying forms of intelligence. The idea that there are multiple forms (domains) of intelligence is potentially problematic because within a single domain, students' levels of intelligence can vary. Most learning tasks require students to draw on a range of intelligences to complete the task. In addition, the idea that intelligence is fixed can lead to teachers failing to provide challenging work for students with lower levels of perceived intelligence. In addition, viewing intelligence as fixed can limit students' view of their own abilities and future learning potential.

KEY RESEARCH

This section presents the key research that critiques learning styles and the concept of multiple intelligences.

Learning styles

A belief in the value of learning styles theory has existed despite the prominent critiques of this theory. Research has found that many teachers across the world agreed individuals learn better when they receive information in their preferred modality (Howard-Jones, 2014). Some academics have attempted to account for the popularity of learning styles theory (Riener and Willingham, 2010), but there is clear psychological evidence that there are no benefits for learning from attempting to present information to learners in their preferred learning style (Geake, 2008; Howard-Jones, 2014; Pashler et al., 2009; Riener and Willingham, 2010). Coffield (2012) argues that 'in short, the research field of learning styles is theoretically incoherent and conceptually confused' (p220). There is an absence of a unified and comprehensive theory and there is a lack of agreed technical vocabulary to underpin this theory. These shortcomings essentially weaken the theory.

The field of learning styles theory is incoherent and conceptually flawed (Coffield et al., 2004a, 2004b). The sheer number of dichotomies that the different models present, as well as the overlap between them, illustrates the lack of a unified theory. Ivie (2009) highlights how John Dewey rejected binary thinking (either/or thinking), which creates false dichotomies, and that in reality, sharp distinctions do not exist (e.g. activists/reflectors). There is no agreed technical vocabulary and no agreed theory to underpin the dichotomies (Coffield et al., 2004a, 2004b). Additionally, learning styles theory has become commercialised. The growth of the learning styles industry (Coffield et al., 2004a, 2004b) and the excessive number of models available serve to reduce the credibility of this theory. Coffield (2012) argues that the existence of 70 learning style instruments demonstrates the disorganised nature of learning styles. Without an agreed model or agreed vocabulary, this creates confusion among educators who are responsible for meeting the needs of their students.

Learning styles are assigned on the basis of an individual completing an assessment tool on which they make generalisations about how they might respond to specific challenges. However, individuals may not be able to provide a definitive response in relation to their learning behaviour; their responses may be socially desirable responses and they may feel constrained by the predetermined format of the assessment tool (Coffield et al., 2004a, 2004b). Coffield (2012), in his critique of learning style assessment tools, argues that context largely shapes how we behave. As individuals respond to various daily challenges, they will be required to draw on a range of modalities, and this undermines a theory that suggests there is a dominant learning style. The statements on learning style assessment tools are often decontextualised. One example of this is highlighted by Sternberg (1999) using the following example: 'When faced with a problem, I like to solve it in a traditional way'. When faced with this statement, the reader must make a response based on the limited range of information given. In this example, it is not clear what type of problem is being referred to in this statement. Additionally, there is no reference to the context in which the problem has developed. The context can largely influence how people respond to problems. For example, problems in the workplace may need to be addressed differently to problems that arise within friendships, relationships or educational contexts. Some problems can be addressed individually. Others may need to be addressed collectively. However, the statement assumes that the problem should be addressed by an individual rather than a larger collective. It is not clear to the reader what is meant by a 'traditional' response to a problem, and it could be argued that some problems require an innovative rather than a 'traditional' solution (Coffield et al., 2004a, 2004b). Far too much is left to interpretation, and the reader is left to make a choice from a predetermined list on the basis of this interpretation, although it is highly unlikely that there will be a single way of solving a problem. However, the question nevertheless implies that this is the case. These arguments weaken the credibility of learning styles theory.

It is important for students to know how to enhance their learning by drawing on a wide range of modalities (Coffield et al., 2004a, 2004b), essentially because students need to use different modalities to complete different kinds of tasks. Effective learners use a range of learning styles rather than relying predominantly on one preferred style. According to Coffield et al. (2004a, 2004b), there is no substantial evidence that matching learning style to tasks (matching hypothesis) increases educational attainment. In fact, evidence from empirical matching studies is contradictory (Coffield et al., 2004a, 2004b). It is therefore unwise to base pedagogical decisions upon inconclusive research evidence. Coffield et al. (2004a, 2004b) argue that learning styles can artificially restrict students' learning experience by limiting the channels through which learning takes place. Learning styles theory also leads to the assumption that learners have a fixed style of learning which is static (Coffield et al., 2004a, 2004b). This is an unwise assumption for both teachers and students because it limits the opportunities for learning.

According to Garner (2000), it is not clear whether Kolb is arguing for learning style traits or states. Therefore, it is unclear if Kolb was promoting the concept of learning styles or four stages of learning (Bergsteiner et al., 2010). There is, however, a substantial body of literature that has emphasised the usefulness of Kolb's theory (Abbey et al., 1985; Kruzich et al., 1986; Nulty and Barrett, 1996; Raschick et al., 1998). Bjork and Bjork (2011) refer to one common assumption on which learning styles theory is based. Learning styles theory assumes that keeping learning constant and predictable will improve later retention. However, they found that varying the types of tasks that learners complete, as well as varying the learning context, in fact improves retention of knowledge and skills.

CASE STUDY

A primary school integrated visual, auditory and kinaesthetic approaches into lessons so that all children had opportunities to learn using these three channels. Teacher explanations were combined with visual modelling. This enabled teachers to demonstrate subject-specific knowledge, concepts and skills. All children had frequent opportunities to learn through rich first-hand experiences. They worked as scientists, historians, geographers, artists and designers. This gave them an opportunity to practise subject-specific skills. During investigative learning, teachers used direct instruction to enable children to make sense of their exploration.

Multiple intelligences

Charles Darwin was the first psychologist to measure intelligence directly, and during the early twentieth century prominent psychologists developed a series of tests designed to measure intelligence (Binet and Simon, 1916; Terman, 1916; Thurstone, 1938).

Traditional intelligence, aptitude and achievement tests had overemphasised logical and linguistic capacities (Gardner and Hatch, 1989). Logical-mathematical and linguistic skills were (and to a certain extent still are) predominantly the way through which intelligence was evaluated. This marginalises those learners who struggle with these aspects of the curriculum. IQ testing is one way of measuring general intelligence. Although the value of these tests has been disputed in the academic literature (Strydom and Du Plessis, 2000), other research has pointed out that they provide a useful indication of a child's general cognitive abilities (Nettelbeck and Wilson, 2005).

However, theorists (Gardner, 1983, 1999) envisaged cognitive abilities as several forms of intelligence that are unrelated, rather than viewing general intelligence as an indication of cognitive ability. Despite these early advances in measuring intelligence, the work of Gardner later in the twentieth century (Gardner, 1975, 1982) began to challenge traditional views of intellect, which had emphasised how specific aspects of brain functioning were part of a single 'semiotic function' (Gardner and Hatch, 1989, p5). Research in the latter part of the twentieth century had suggested that the human mind was modular and that distinct psychological processes were evident when dealing with different kinds of mental functions (Gardner and Wolf, 1983; Gardner et al., 1974). There is now a consensus that intelligence represents an 'ability to understand complex ideas, to adapt effectively to the environment, to learn from experience, [and] to engage in various forms of reasoning to overcome obstacles by taking thought' (Neisser et al., 1996, p77).

Gardner was concerned that this narrow measure of intelligence promoted by the traditional intelligence theorists failed to recognise that human activity draws on multiple domains of intelligence. Gardner developed a broader definition of intelligence that included problem-solving and practical forms of intelligence. He saw the human intelligences as relatively distinct. Thus, intelligence in one domain was not dependent on intelligence in another domain. In collaboration with his colleagues, Gardner carried out a systematic literature review on human intelligence. They examined the cognitive capacities of typically developing individuals as well as the cognitive capacities of prodigies, atypically developing individuals and savants. They found that individuals differ in their intelligence profiles and that there was no inevitable association between any two intelligences.

Multiple Intelligence (MI) theory was introduced by Gardner in his book *Frames of Mind* (Gardner, 1983). Initially, Gardner concluded that there were seven intelligences (linguistic, logical-mathematical, musical, spatial, bodily-kinaesthetic, intrapersonal, interpersonal), and in 1995 he added an eighth intelligence (naturalistic). The assumption of the theory is that the intelligences are independent of each other and individuals often demonstrate an uneven profile in that some intelligences will be greater than others. In contrast, standard intelligence tests demonstrate a bias towards logical and linguistic skills. The assessment of intelligence using these tests is carried out artificially by removing a child from the social context in which learning takes place. Conversely, assessment of multiple intelligences is not decontextualised and takes place within a familiar social and cultural context (Gardner and Hatch, 1989) in which learning takes place, thus making the assessment more authentic. Almeida (2010) has argued that standard intelligence tests currently used in psychology are not significantly different to those used a century ago. This is despite advances in socio-constructivist learning theory, which has emphasised the importance of learning through dialogue within social and cultural contexts. Despite these developments within learning theory, a psychometric approach to testing intelligence is still the dominant approach (Almeida, 2010). The psychometric tests present items in an abstract manner and terminology is often vague and generalised. Gardner's work on intelligence presents an alternative to the dominant psychometric approaches. Assessment of intelligence takes place within classroom contexts, and therefore the assessment has greater ecological validity than standard psychometric tests (Almeida, 2010). Intelligence relates to the ability to undertake a wide variety of problem-solving tasks, the ability to think in an abstract manner and the ability to infer relationships, thus highlighting the multidimensional nature of intelligence (Almeida, 2010). In addition, different individuals pursue different goals, and therefore it seems logical to argue that there are many different types of intelligence (White, 2006).

Gardner's theory has several important applications; these include planning schemes of work that span all the intelligences, providing intervention programmes in areas of weakness or enrichment programmes in areas of strength for learners with special educational needs or gifted students (Klein, 1997). In addition, the theory challenges those schools that currently overemphasise logical-mathematical and linguistic knowledge to adapt the pedagogical approaches that are adopted so that the different intelligences are reflected in models of curriculum delivery.

However, MI theory has been critiqued. According to White (2005), 'putting children into boxes that have not been proved to exist may end up restricting the education they receive, leading teachers to overly rigid views of individual pupils' potentialities, and, what is worse, a new type of stereotyping' (p9). Multiple intelligence theory has been rejected outright by researchers that support psychometric approaches to measuring intelligence (Brand, 1996; Sternberg, 1983), with some claiming that Gardner's intelligences are styles of cognition rather than intelligences per se

(Morgan, 1992). Although Gardner has emphasised that separate intelligences work largely independently, most activities tend to draw on several intelligences (Klein, 1997). Nettelbeck and Wilson (2005) emphasise that Gardner's separate intelligences overlap rather than exist independently. For example, Klein (1997) highlights that conversation draws on both interpersonal and linguistic intelligences. Although Gardner has emphasised that pairs of intelligences may overlap or be correlated in some way, this weakens his claim for categorising the intelligences as distinct entities. If intelligence systems work together in practice, then this could in fact support the notion of one general intelligence and that abilities in specific areas are merely components of this intelligence.

Although Gardner cites examples of geniuses, many of these geniuses excel in more than one intelligence domain and within a subset of a domain rather than demonstrating high performance throughout a single domain (Klein, 1997). Additionally, many geniuses do not fit the categories of Gardner's intelligences, and given that geniuses are rare, these examples are unhelpful as a basis for educational practice (Klein, 1997). This weakens Gardner's work. For example, Gardner discusses savants – individuals who do one thing very well. However, Klein challenges this by pointing out that these individuals do not usually excel across a whole intelligence domain (Klein, 1997). Klein uses the example of hyperlexic autistic readers who can decode print well but have poor comprehension; therefore, they do not have high overall linguistic intelligence. Children with dyslexia may have good listening comprehension or oracy skills but also experience significant difficulties in the skill of phonological processing; therefore, they may not necessarily demonstrate a weakness across the entire domain of linguistic intelligence. Some students may have particular strengths in solving calculations but demonstrate poor spatial awareness, thus demonstrating an uneven profile across the domain of logical-mathematical intelligence. Furthermore, Gardner's model relates achievement in specific areas to intelligence, in contrast to traditional views of intelligence, which focus on cognitive thought processes. However, the linking of intelligence to achievement is problematic because it suggests that this achievement will have relative stability over time (Klein, 1997). However, achievements can decline over a period of time, particularly if skills are not practised. In contrast, cognitive thought processes have relative stability over time, and this raises questions about whether intelligence should be defined on the basis of specific abilities, skills and talents, rather than on the basis of an individual's cognitive thought processes.

A significant limitation of Gardner's theory is that students who score low in a specific intelligence might avoid activities that draw on this intelligence, even though they might learn through investing effort into a domain (Covington, 1992; Palmquist and Young, 1992). Additionally, students might choose to disengage with activities that they find challenging (Klein, 1997). Klein emphasises that reliable methods for assessing the different intelligences in Gardner's theory have not been established and that the categories are too broad to be useful. Gardner fails to provide empirical evidence to support his theory (Waterhouse, 2006). Gardner also fails to provide a set of subcomponents that can be tested for each domain of intelligence (Waterhouse, 2006). The various intelligences are described by general characteristics rather than specific components, and this has prevented researchers from conducting rigorous tests to explore the validity of his theory (Waterhouse, 2006). Gardner assumed that the theory required no empirical validation because the theory is based on a synthesis of research findings. However, multiple intelligence theory merely assumes the validity of the intelligences because there is no rigorous way of actually testing these (Waterhouse, 2006).

Coffield et al. (2004a, 2004b) argue that research evidence on formative assessment (Black and Wiliam, 1998) is academically robust, so it would be better for educators to concentrate on developing this aspect of their practice rather than focusing on learning styles theory, which has no agreed theoretical base and no robust assessment procedure to underpin the various models. Learner feedback is critical in promoting learning by accelerating achievement (Black and Wiliam, 1998), but there is no evidence from research that justifies dividing learners into learning style groups. Theories of multiple intelligence also lack empirical justification because there is no agreed tool for measuring intelligence within each domain. Additionally, learners are unlikely to excel across a whole domain and are more likely to demonstrate strengths in specific aspects of a domain. Different tasks require different abilities, and therefore it seems illogical to group learners using artificial constructs. Both theories categorise students either on the basis of learning style or intelligence, and these categories place restrictions on students that can be detrimental to learning. Effective learners use a range of different styles of learning and abilities in different tasks, and therefore it seems more logical for educators to ensure that they use a wide range of teaching strategies, as well as providing students with access to a broad, rich curriculum. This will enable them to develop their interests and skills in different disciplines.

Intelligence as a fixed trait

Research demonstrates that two individuals with differing mindsets can start out at the same academic level, but over time the individual with the growth mindset will begin to outperform the individual with the fixed mindset (Dweck, 2009). Blackwell et al. (2007) found that throughout the duration of a two-year study, adolescent students with a fixed mindset did not show any improvement in their academic achievements. However, the achievements of the students that had been identified as having a growth mindset did show improvement. Research demonstrates that students who have a growth mindset achieve significantly better grades than their peers with a fixed mindset (Aronson et al., 2001; Blackwell et al., 2007).

CASE STUDY

A secondary school promoted the concept of growth mindset in all lessons. Students were aware that hard work, effort and persistence could improve their intelligence. They knew that intelligence was not a fixed trait. This approach was particularly effective in assessment and feedback. Students were encouraged to view all feedback as developmental in that it was designed to help them improve. If students received a low grade, they were taught to use this as an opportunity to invest greater effort and persistence in their studies so that they could improve their grade. The school culture promoted the message that learning is hard and that mistakes are inevitable. However, the culture of growth mindset meant that students could recover from perceived failures. Teachers talked openly with students about which aspects of a subject they found difficult and they shared their own experiences of perceived educational failures with the students. In this way, the teachers acted as powerful role models to students, and this encouraged students to work hard and invest greater effort into their work.

── NEXT STEPS ──

In your teaching, promote the following messages:

- With hard work and effort, you will grow your mental capacity.
- It is never too late to stop learning.
- You might find something difficult right now, but with effort and perseverance you will grasp it.
- There are different ways of showing your intelligence. People are intelligent in different ways.
- Your intelligence is not fixed; you can develop it by working hard.

In your teaching, integrate a variety of visual, auditory and kinaesthetic approaches so that for all students, learning is reinforced through all of these channels.

What have you learned?

This chapter has addressed common myths in relation to our understanding of learning styles and intelligence. It has presented psychological evidence to support you to challenge the existing research in relation to learning styles. In doing so, it has emphasised that the evidence demonstrates there are no benefits for learners in having information presented to them through their preferred style. It has also argued that the commercialisation of learning styles theory has been problematic and has created confusion among educators in relation to credibility and impact. The chapter then offered a case study to illustrate some effective practice and to encourage you to reflect on your current professional approaches. Additionally, the chapter has presented literature and research to demonstrate how our understanding of intelligence has been challenged in recent years. Through this discussion, we have addressed common myths in relation to multiple types of intelligence and the concept of fixed intelligence. Case study material has been provided to highlight the implications of these assumptions in relation to our teaching and to support your understanding of effective practice.

── FURTHER READING ──

Brand, C. (1996) *The G Factor: General Intelligence and Its Implications*. New York: John Wiley.

Brown, A. and Kaminske, A. (2018) *Five Teaching and Learning Myths – Debunked*. London: Routledge.

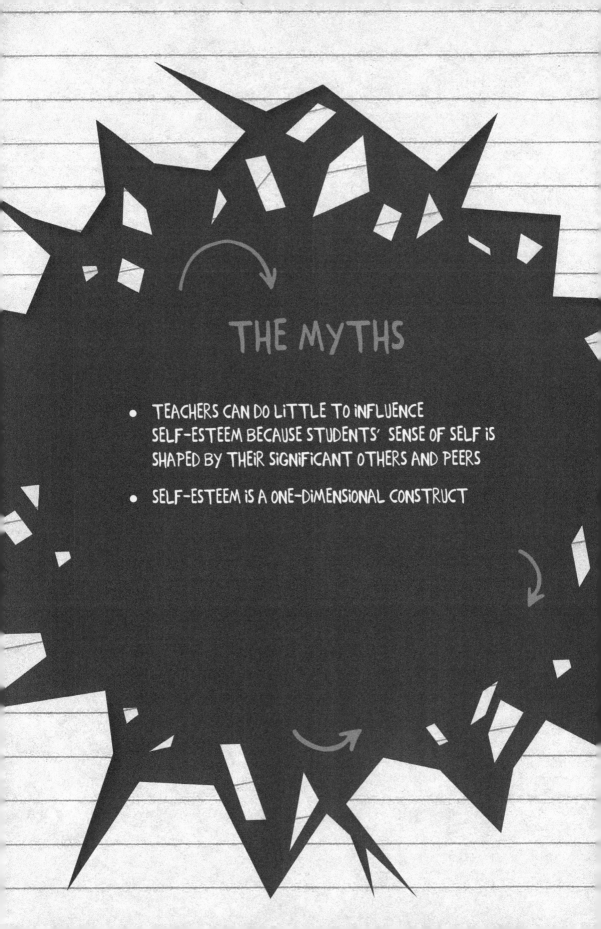

THE MYTHS

- TEACHERS CAN DO LITTLE TO INFLUENCE SELF-ESTEEM BECAUSE STUDENTS' SENSE OF SELF IS SHAPED BY THEIR SIGNIFICANT OTHERS AND PEERS

- SELF-ESTEEM IS A ONE-DIMENSIONAL CONSTRUCT

2
SELF-ESTEEM

What will you learn?

This chapter introduces you to theoretical perspectives on self-esteem. It identifies self-esteem as a two-dimensional construct that is made up of self-worth and self-competence (Mruk, 1999). It identifies the factors that may influence students' self-esteem and outlines some practical implications for schools.

WHAT ARE THE MYTHS?

- Teachers can do little to influence self-esteem because students' sense of self is shaped by their significant others and peers.
- Self-esteem is a one-dimensional construct.

Why should teachers challenge the myths?

The idea that teachers are unable to influence a student's self-esteem is potentially dangerous because students with low self-esteem can develop 'learned helplessness' (Maier and Seligman, 1967). This is a state of passivity following prolonged exposure to adverse situations. Therefore, if a student is continually made to feel, through their interactions with others, that they are worthless as a person and not capable of achieving anything, they will begin to internalise these feelings. Teachers can play a crucial role in changing a student's appraisal of themselves, but the longer they experience negative feelings in relation to their sense of self, the more internalised these feelings become as they develop (Jindal-Snape and Miller, 2010).

KEY RESEARCH

Since 1967, the seminal work of Coopersmith (1967) has made a significant and lasting contribution to the body of work on self-esteem. Coopersmith (1967) defined self-esteem as 'a personal judgement of worthiness' (pp4-5), in line with others who also focused on self-worth as being a key component of self-esteem (Rogers, 1961). In contrast, other academics focused more on self-competence in their explanations of self-esteem (White, 1963).

These varying perspectives on self-esteem led Mruk (1999) to develop a two-dimensional model of self-esteem that includes both self-worth and self-competence. Self-worth relates to an individual's holistic evaluation of themselves ('I am a good person'). Individuals form this view based on the feedback they receive from others, including significant others, peers and teachers. Therefore, other people's evaluations of our worthiness influence the view that we form of ourselves. The second dimension, self-competence, refers to an individual's overall ability ('I am able to meet the challenges I face in life'). Although self-competence is domain-specific (i.e. we can be more competent at some things than others), Mruk was interested in an individual's overall appraisal of their self-competence rather than a differentiated evaluation of it.

According to Mruk (1999), an individual with low self-worth and low self-competence will have classic low self-esteem. These individuals tend to have a negative perception of their own abilities and self-worth and may have low expectations of themselves. In relation to students, those with classic low self-esteem may be reluctant to contribute in class, may easily disengage, and may also demonstrate signs of poor mental health. In contrast, students who score highly in both domains will display high self-esteem. They tend to engage with most tasks and demonstrate high levels of motivation. These students do not usually anticipate failure.

Individuals can also demonstrate an uneven profile across both domains. Some may demonstrate high self-worth but low self-competence. These students may have received positive evaluations or appraisals from significant others and peers that may have created a positive sense of self-worth. However, their self-competence may be lower because they may struggle to perform age-appropriate tasks when asked to do so. These students may demonstrate task avoidance strategies and may also demonstrate denial about their own competence.

Some students may demonstrate a positive sense of self-competence based on their previous experiences of success. However, experiences of traumatic events, other forms of adversity, and exposure to negative appraisals from significant others and peers may result in these individuals demonstrating antisocial behaviour and more serious forms of deviance.

Mruk's model illustrates the duality of self-esteem, and it is probably the most comprehensive explanation to date (Jindal-Snape and Miller, 2010). Literature has also differentiated between global self-esteem and domain-specific self-esteem. Global self-esteem refers to an individual's overall evaluation of themselves and is likely to influence non-academic outcomes, including well-being and motivation. Individuals with high global self-esteem have a positive view of themselves but those with low global self-esteem have an unfavourable self-view. In contrast, domain-specific or differentiated self-esteem is positively associated with academic outcomes (Pullmann and Allik, 2008). The domain-specific perspective acknowledges that individuals can have varying levels of self-esteem in different domains ('I am good at English but not mathematics'). Our self-esteem can fluctuate, and individuals can also become defensive when they feel that their self-esteem is being threatened.

The importance of self-esteem

High self-esteem acts as a buffer in that it enables individuals to cope with setbacks (Jindal-Snape and Miller, 2010). Those with low self-esteem respond more negatively to setbacks. This can result in them disengaging from future challenges and giving up on their education. In contrast, those with high self-esteem tend to be more resilient (Jindal-Snape and Miller, 2010). They persist with challenges and request support to help them overcome obstacles.

CASE STUDY

A primary school identified a group of children who had poor self-esteem but were also displaying signs of conduct disorder. They demonstrated a broad range of behaviours, including disengaging in lessons, shouting at teachers, refusing to complete tasks, and verbally and physically assaulting other children. With the support of an educational psychologist, the school introduced solution-focused coaching to try to improve their self-worth. Essentially, the strategy involves a series of positive conversations with young people through which realistic goals are identified and previous negative perceptions of the self are reframed. Specific strategies included:

- *Scaling*: Children are asked to rate their behaviour, confidence, resilience, team-working or motivation on a scale of 0-10. The conversation then focuses on what the child is doing right to achieve that score. The child subsequently identifies what point on the scale they would like to reach within a specific time frame. The conversation then focuses on what the child will be doing differently to achieve the target score.
- *Complimenting*: Finding things about which to compliment the child.
- *Exception-finding*: These conversations focus on when the child is demonstrating exceptions to their usual behaviour (e.g. 'Tell me about a time when you stayed calm in a difficult situation').
- *Problem free talk*: These conversations focus on the child's strengths and interests both inside and outside school.

After seven weeks, the targeted children demonstrated signs of improved self-worth. Their behaviour was still not perfect, but there was a reduction in the number of incidents that were recorded. The school decided to continue with the approach.

Contributing factors

Our self-worth is influenced by the quality of our relationships with others, their overall appraisal of us, and the evaluations we make on ourselves. Therefore, teachers play an important role in shaping how students view themselves. Teachers are in a unique position to directly influence students' self-worth. However, the earlier this occurs within a child's development, the more impact it will have. This is because feelings of low self-worth can become internalised over time and 'learned helplessness' (Maier and Seligman, 1967) can become established. As students develop their abilities in specific domains, particularly in secondary school, this will improve their sense of self-competence, and in turn this will contribute to improved overall self-esteem.

The loss of significant relationships can impact detrimentally on self-esteem (Jindal-Snape and Miller, 2010), particularly self-worth. Students may receive positive feedback from others, but if these relationships are lost or damaged, their self-worth can also be damaged. Young people who have lost significant others in their lives can be adversely affected, particularly if they have lost a parent. Refugees or asylum seekers may have lost contact with family members or experienced significant trauma, and this can impact detrimentally on their self-worth. In addition, children who are exposed to adverse experiences in the home or in their community may also experience low self-esteem. This includes children who have suffered abuse, neglect and parental conflict. Children who are looked after or those who did not form secure attachments with their primary carer (usually the mother) may experience feelings of rejection that can negatively affect their sense of self-worth.

Child maltreatment can severely impact the healthy development of the self. Researchers have found that child abuse is associated with low self-esteem, low self-compassion and external locus of control (Bolger and Patterson, 2001; Eskin, 2012; Tanaka et al., 2011). Self-compassion relates to the care that an individual provides for themselves. Someone with an external locus of control feels that they have no control over situations that affect them, and they are therefore influenced by external factors. This contrasts with an individual who has an internal locus of control. These individuals retain a strong sense of control over their own lives. Low self-esteem, low self-compassion, and an external locus of control lead to increased risk of emotional dysregulation, suicidal ideation, anxiety and depression. Damage to the various self-constructs listed can occur from a very young age and the negative consequences can persist throughout adulthood.

Transitions can be a difficult time for young people (Jindal-Snape and Miller, 2010), particularly when they change class or school. Children with high overall self-esteem usually feel more able to cope with the challenges associated with transitions. Their positive evaluation of their self-competence acts as a buffer and makes them more resilient. Children with low self-esteem may have less resilience during times of transition and they may require greater support.

When children transfer to secondary school, their evaluation of their self-competence can change both positively and negatively. The transition to secondary school usually signals a different approach to teaching. Students may be learning different subjects to those that they studied at primary school and the approach to teaching is often very different. The structure of the day is also very different. If students struggle with the secondary curriculum, this can negatively affect their sense of self-competence. Conversely, if they enjoy the subjects that they are learning and perform well in these, this can positively affect their self-competence. Students will be exposed to a broader range of teachers in secondary school, unlike in primary schools, where they can develop a strong relationship with a single teacher. Lack of exposure to a single teacher can negatively impact on young people's self-worth.

CASE STUDY

A secondary school introduced a term-long bridging project for the Year 6 children in the feeder primary schools. The project focused on the theme of climate change and was taught by the geography teacher from the secondary school. The children completed a range of cross-curricular activities. Some of the lessons were taught in the primary school, but midway through the unit the

3

MOTIVATION

What will you learn?

In this chapter, you will learn about different types of motivation, both intrinsic and extrinsic. This chapter also introduces Dweck's concept of growth mindset and its association with motivation and achievement. The concept of 'grit' is also introduced. This chapter argues that there is value in promoting the concept of a growth mindset with students. It argues that this is likely to increase student motivation and achievement. There is also value in supporting students to invest sustained effort towards long-term goals. This promotes intrinsic rather than extrinsic motivation. The links between motivation, learned helplessness and external locus of control are clear. These concepts have been discussed in Chapter 2. This chapter argues that fixed mindsets can reduce student motivation, decrease engagement, and lead to students not achieving their full potential.

WHAT ARE THE MYTHS?

- Intellectual ability is more important than grit.
- Intellectual ability is a fixed characteristic.
- Students who demonstrate an orientation towards performance-related goals perform better than those who have an orientation towards mastery goals.

Why should teachers challenge the myths?

One of the key approaches suggested in this chapter to increase students' motivation is to develop within students a belief that intelligence can grow and be developed through effort. If students develop a view that intelligence is static, they can easily start to become demotivated. Motivation is enhanced through achievement. Students achieve well when they are prepared to invest effort into their learning and if they demonstrate resilience when working on challenging tasks. If students believe that they will never improve, then they can very quickly start to become demotivated. If they start to understand that the brain is malleable and easily susceptible to influences from the environment (e.g. education), then they are more likely to be motivated because this perspective offers them a sense of hope. Effort and resilience are critical to achievement, even for students who demonstrate high levels of intellectual ability.

KEY RESEARCH

Research demonstrates that improving achievement enhances motivation and confidence. It has been argued that:

Teachers who are confronted with the poor motivation and confidence of low attaining students may interpret this as the cause of their low attainment and assume that it is both necessary and possible to address their motivation before attempting to teach them new material. In fact, the evidence shows that attempts to enhance motivation in this way are unlikely to achieve that end. Even if they do, the impact on subsequent learning is close to zero ... the poor motivation of low attainers is a logical response to repeated failure. Start getting them to succeed and their motivation and confidence should increase.

(Coe et al., 2014, p23)

Promoting grit

Research on 'grit' (Duckworth, 2017; Duckworth et al., 2007) suggests that this is an important characteristic which influences achievement. The term is sometimes used interchangeably with resilience. However, there are some key differences between grit and resilience. Resilience is usually used to describe overcoming situations of adversity, although this is not uncontroversial (see Roffey, 2017). In contrast, grit is associated with sustained perseverance (Duckworth et al., 2007) towards long-term goals. Research demonstrates that grit is essential to high achievement, and seminal research has found that grit is more predictive of high achievement than IQ (Terman and Oden, 1947). Individuals with grit are able to stay focused on achieving long-term goals, even in the absence of instant gratification. They demonstrate a very high level of ability to stay focused on achieving their goals and are motivated by the accomplishment of the task they are undertaking rather than extrinsic rewards.

Types of motivation

According to Ryan and Deci (2000), 'the most basic distinction is between intrinsic motivation, which refers to doing something because it is inherently interesting or enjoyable, and extrinsic motivation, which refers to doing something because it leads to a separable outcome' (p55). A child is extrinsically motivated when they respond positively to external reinforcers. Thus, they do not complete a task because they are motivated to do so; they complete it to gain the external reward. Seminal research has demonstrated that children start school with a high level of intrinsic motivation but the level of intrinsic motivation declines as they get older (Middleton and Spanias, 1999), possibly because the subject content they are expected to learn or the tasks they are required to complete become less interesting. However, extrinsic motivators do not always work. Research demonstrates that students who are not intrinsically motivated to complete a task may not respond positively to external motivators (Ryan and Deci, 2006).

Students' goals also affect motivation and performance. Goals can be broadly divided into either mastery or performance goals (Ryan and Deci, 2000). Mastery goals are evident when students have a desire to complete a task to gain knowledge and skills. Students with a high degree of intrinsic motivation tend to demonstrate mastery goals. In contrast, students with high levels of extrinsic motivation demonstrate performance goals. In addition, students who are motivated by performance goals tend to display high levels of extrinsic motivation and low levels of intrinsic motivation. Students with a mastery goal orientation tended to have greater levels of intrinsic motivation and low levels of extrinsic motivation (Spinath and Steinmayr, 2012).

Research shows that students who demonstrate mastery goals tend to outperform those with a performance goal orientation (Middleton and Spanias, 1999). This suggests that teachers should focus on fostering intrinsic motivation in students through making subject content meaningful, interesting and relevant so that they become deeply absorbed in it. This will support students to develop a mastery goal orientation.

CASE STUDY

A secondary school had a large number of students who were motivated by performance goals. They were motivated to complete courses to gain qualifications and they demonstrated very high levels of competition between each other. Teachers had been promoting this competitive climate for several years. Many of the students did not continue studying the subjects beyond their qualifications and many progressed into further and higher education to study completely different courses to those they had studied at school. The school decided to focus on changing students' goal orientation by creating stimulating units of work that were relevant and meaningful, as well as addressing contemporary issues. Teachers focused on immersing students in rich learning experiences rather than on teaching solely to examination specifications. The students became intrinsically motivated by the subjects that they were studying in school and many continued to study these subjects in further and higher education. The climate of competition was replaced by collaboration, which was fostered through exciting project-based team learning.

Promoting a growth mindset

Research demonstrates that the brain can physically change and that this can occur well into adulthood (Abiola and Dhindsa, 2012). Research undertaken by Maguire et al. (2006) examined the physical changes in the brain in individuals undertaking training to become London taxi drivers. The research demonstrated that following the training, there was a significant growth in the hippocampus, the area of the brain which processes spatial information (Maguire et al., 2006). Research that demonstrates the plasticity of the brain supports the belief that intellectual ability can be enhanced and developed through learning (Sternberg, 2005). It therefore supports the idea of a 'growth mindset' (Dweck, 1999). People with growth mindsets believe that intelligence can grow and be developed through effort. In contrast, those with fixed mindsets view intelligence as a static trait, not something that can be developed.

Dweck (2007, 2009) argued that mindsets play a critical role in the motivation and achievement of learners. Learners with a fixed mindset can easily give up when learning becomes too challenging. Conversely, learners with a growth mindset embrace learning opportunities that provide a challenge, even where failure is a very real possibility (Dweck, 2007). Although two individuals with differing mindsets can start out achieving similar levels academically, research suggests that over time, the individual with the growth mindset will begin to outperform the individual with the fixed mindset (Dweck, 2009). Research demonstrates that 'at every socioeconomic level, those who hold more of a growth mindset consistently outperform those who do not' (Claro et al., 2016, p8667).

Fixed-ability thinking can encourage inequality (Boaler, 2013) because individuals with fixed mindsets may lack motivation and resilience and may not be prepared to invest effort into developing their brain. In the worst cases, these individuals give up on learning and develop 'learned helplessness' (see Chapter 2).

The attitudes of teachers towards intelligence and school culture play an important role in how students view themselves. The use of ability groupings in schools promotes the idea of a fixed mindset (Boaler, 2015). Boaler (2015) has argued that ability groupings transmit to students the view that some students are not capable of completing more challenging tasks, thus suggesting intelligence is static. Static groups are common in schools; the opportunity to change groups is limited (Davies et al., 2003; Dixon, 2002) and research suggests that most pupils remain in the same ability group for the duration of their school career (Ollerton, 2001). This promotes the idea of a fixed mindset, which is transmitted to students.

Dweck (2010) suggests that the culture and learning approaches within schools could help students to change their approach to learning and encourage the development of growth mindset beliefs. A shift in culture may require teachers to reframe their perceptions of intelligence and for schools to review the use of fixed-ability groups.

CASE STUDY

A primary school developed a culture that embraced the principles of the growth mindset. When children found tasks difficult and they displayed signs of learned helplessness, teachers responded by making the following points:

- 'Learning is hard. I sometimes find new learning difficult.'
- 'If your brain is hurting, it means that you are learning.'
- 'You might not be able to do it yet, but you will be able to do it soon.'
- 'Keep trying and you will understand it.'

These positive messages improved children's self-efficacy, as well as their resilience, determination and grit.

NEXT STEPS

Find out which students in your class are intrinsically or extrinsically motivated. Some students may respond to both motivators. Reflect on how you can support all students to be more intrinsically motivated.

What have you learned?

In this chapter, you have been introduced to key theoretical perspectives on motivation. You have learned that the development of a growth mindset supports motivation. You have also learned about the relationship between students' goal orientations, their motivation and their academic performance. You have also learned about the importance of investing sustained effort into achieving long-term goals, and that this has greater impact on achievement than IQ.

FURTHER READING

Dweck, C.S. (2006) *Mindset: The New Psychology of Success*. New York: Ballantine Books.

Dweck, C.S. (2010) Even geniuses work hard. *Educational Leadership*, 68(1): 16–20.

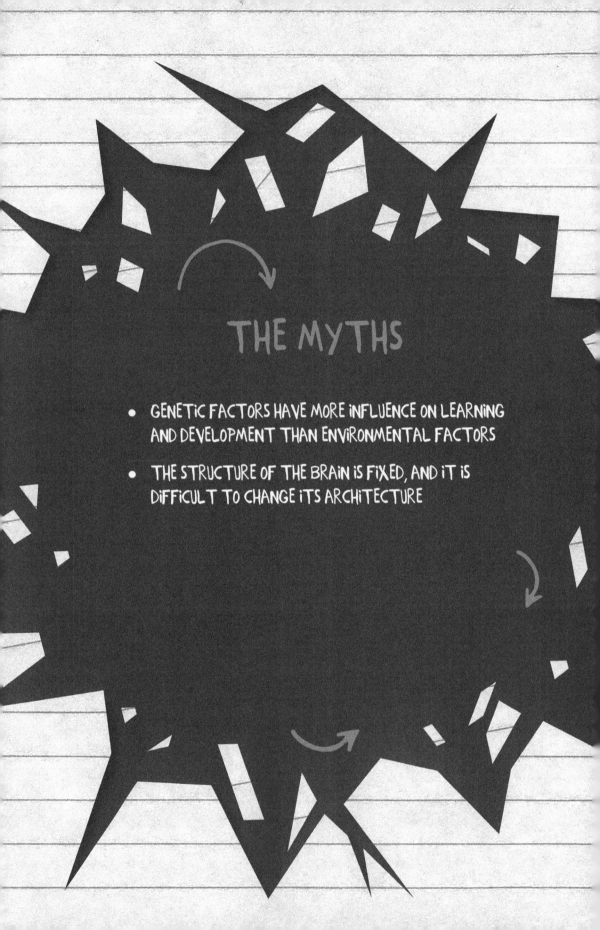

THE MYTHS

- GENETIC FACTORS HAVE MORE INFLUENCE ON LEARNING AND DEVELOPMENT THAN ENVIRONMENTAL FACTORS

- THE STRUCTURE OF THE BRAIN IS FIXED, AND IT IS DIFFICULT TO CHANGE ITS ARCHITECTURE

4

HOW CHILDREN LEARN

What will you learn?

This chapter introduces you to some of the latest research findings into how children learn. It examines the factors that affect brain development and introduces you to the concept of schema. It explores the role of social processes in learning and argues that children's learning is not just influenced by individual factors, but also by interactions with others in social and cultural contexts. Metacognition and cognitive load theory are also addressed.

WHAT ARE THE MYTHS?

- Genetic factors have more influence on learning and development than environmental factors.
- The structure of the brain is fixed, and it is difficult to change its architecture.

Why should teachers challenge the myths?

These assumptions about the brain can limit the potential of individuals, particularly if they believe that their intelligence is largely determined by their genes. If genetic factors are thought to have a greater influence on an individual's capacity to learn and on their intelligence, this can lead to disengagement from the process of learning, low self-esteem and lack of aspiration. If teachers believe that they can do little to influence the structure of the brain, this can result in low teacher expectations of specific students. These are dangerous assumptions and do not reflect current knowledge about learning and development.

KEY RESEARCH

The evidence from research has demonstrated that:

- Children's learning and development is shaped by a combination of environmental factors and learning opportunities both inside and outside schools.
- Learning involves physical, psychological, social and emotional processes. These influence one another in that the interactions between these processes can enable or restrict learning.
- The brain and intelligence are malleable and can be changed by environmental influences, including exposure to high-quality teaching.
- Our experiences activate neural pathways that enable new ways of thinking and new skills to develop.
- Emotions and social contexts shape neural connections that contribute to attention, concentration and memory, as well as knowledge transfer and application. Research has demonstrated that chronic stress due to trauma affects cognition and working memory.
- Differentiated instruction enables optimum brain growth.

(Darling-Hammond et al., 2019)

Research demonstrates that 'experience is a "stressor" to brain growth – throughout life, interpersonal experiences and relational connections activate neural pathways, generating energy flow through electrical impulses that strengthen connectivity' (Cantor et al., 2019, p311). A combination of both genetic factors and early experiences shape neuronal connections, which develop neural circuits. These enable increasingly complex mental activities to occur (Moore, 2015; Slavich and Cole, 2013). As these circuits become increasingly stable, they contribute to the development of complex thoughts, skills and behaviours in individuals (Cantor et al., 2019). Environmental and interpersonal experiences influence brain growth throughout childhood and well into adulthood. It has been demonstrated that 'genes act as followers, not prime movers, in developmental processes' (Cantor et al., 2019, p309). It has also been demonstrated that positive, nurturing relationships are essential to brain development. These relationships build strong brain architecture (Cantor et al., 2019). We know that children's development is shaped by micro-ecological contexts (i.e. families, peers, schools and communities) as well as macro-ecological contexts (i.e. economic and cultural systems).

The brain is characterised by plasticity rather than stability. Its structure is influenced not just by genetics, but by the micro and macro contexts within which individuals are situated. Physical, psychological, social and emotional processes also influence brain structure. Emotions can have powerful effects on developmental pathways (Cantor et al., 2019). The implications of this are significant because the research demonstrates that an individual's experiences can shape the development of neural pathways which facilitate mental processes. Thus, exposure to high-quality teaching can change the structure of the brain by activating new neural pathways.

Memory

The development of memory is critical to learning. There are two main types of memory: the working memory and the long-term memory. The working memory holds a limited amount of information that is used to execute cognitive tasks. It enables individuals to hold multiple pieces of information that are used to complete a variety of daily tasks. In contrast, the long-term memory stores information indefinitely, including information that is not being used in the working memory. Repetition is required to 'fix' information in the long-term memory, but once it is stored in the long-term memory it can remain there for a significant time.

One of the ways that the brain stores information is through the development of schemas. Schemas are mental structures of frameworks for representing some aspect of the world, including knowledge. Organising knowledge into schemas facilitates its retrieval from the long-term memory. Schemas can be considered to be categories that a child develops through their interactions with the world and with others. For example, a child may develop a schema about dogs. They learn that dogs have four legs and a tail, and they apply this schema to identify dogs when they see one. Schemas continue to develop throughout childhood and into adult life. They are convenient categories for storing information to aid retrieval. One way of thinking about them is to imagine they are storage folders that group together information which fits into a specific category.

Piaget (1952) articulated how new learning occurs using schemas. He used the term 'assimilation' when new information is added to current schemas. In the example above, the child's existing schema (i.e. a dog has four legs and a tail) is applied to different sizes, colours and breeds of dog. The schema still works because the animals are all dogs. Piaget referred to this as a process of 'equilibrium'. However, 'disequilibrium' occurs when new information cannot be fitted into existing schemas. This causes the child to experience what Piaget referred to as 'cognitive dissonance'. This is where schemas are forced to change to 'accommodate' new information. This happens when the existing schema (knowledge) does not work and needs to be changed to deal with a new object or situation. In the same example, the child may see a horse and call it a dog, but then subsequently learns that this is incorrect. The schema no longer works and needs to be changed. The process of reframing a schema can be challenging, but this is when learning occurs. It is the process through which new knowledge is accommodated with existing knowledge to return to a state of equilibrium. The processes of equilibrium and disequilibrium then continue as schemas become increasingly more complex.

NEXT STEPS

The following section outlines the implications of this research for schools and teachers.

Block scheduling

Block scheduling is the practice of timetabling fewer but longer classes per day. This practice is thought to reduce cognitive load and anxiety for students (Darling-Hammond et al., 2019). Cognitive load refers to the amount of mental effort required in using working memory. If students are required to participate in four or five lessons each day, this places a significant load on the working memory. In this instance, students will need to draw on many different neural pathways in the brain as they switch from one lesson to the next. Reducing the number of lessons eases the cognitive load on the working memory and allows teachers to achieve greater depth in relation to subject-specific knowledge, understanding, application and synthesis.

Building on children's knowledge and experiences

Social constructivist perspectives on learning assume that individual capacities develop within social contexts (Vygotsky, 1978). Vygotsky developed the concept of the zone of proximal development. This is the distance between a child's actual level of development and their proximal level (i.e. what they are capable of achieving with the support from a more able peer or adult). Scaffolding is used to support a child to move between the two stages of development, but learning should always be pitched within the zone so that it is always a level above the child's current level of development. Vygotsky was interested in how dialogue (including internal dialogue and dialogue between individuals) promotes learning within social and cultural contexts.

Collaborative learning

Research demonstrates that brain development is experience-dependent (Darling-Hammond et al., 2019). Research has also found that cooperative learning promotes higher achievement compared to individualistic efforts (Johnson et al., 2000). The implications for pedagogy are for teachers to provide rich collaborative learning opportunities through paired work and group work. These opportunities may involve learners working together to solve a problem, complete a task or create a new product. When learners are working together on activities or learning tasks, it is important to ensure that groups are small. This ensures that everyone is able to participate and support a collective task which has been clearly assigned. Learners in the group may work on separate tasks that contribute to an overall goal, or they may work together on a shared task. There are many different approaches to collaborative learning, and these involve different kinds of organisation and task.

The impact of collaborative learning is consistently positive. However, it is essential to plan your approaches carefully in order to maximise impact. Effective collaborative learning is about much more than simply sitting learners together and giving them a group task to complete. Instead, structured approaches should be used with specific and well-designed tasks and activities. If used, any elements of competition must be introduced and monitored carefully. Teachers need to ensure that learners do not focus on competition at the expense of learning. Approaches to collaborative learning that promote communication, dialogue and talk must also be planned specifically and meaningfully.

CASE STUDY

A group of middle leaders dedicated existing professional development time to work together on a common aspect of pedagogy or practice. The leaders agreed that they wanted to use this time to explore how collaborative learning could be used across the school. The leaders began by collecting and discussing existing research in relation to collaborative learning and its impact on learners and their progress.

The middle leaders then created a list of points that they felt needed to be considered and thought about before any collaborative learning approaches could be implemented effectively. In summary, the points that they identified included:

- the need to provide opportunities for students to practise working together (as it does not happen automatically);
- the importance of ensuring that tasks are planned carefully so that learners can work together effectively and efficiently (otherwise, learners may attempt to work on their own);
- the extent to which competition can be used to support learners working together, and the importance of identifying when competition is causing learners to focus on winning rather than learning;
- how the planning of tasks and activities can encourage all pupils to engage in talk and discussion;
- teachers' existing strengths and areas of development, and any training that may be required to ensure that collaborative learning is used appropriately and effectively.

The teachers met at several points throughout the academic year to discuss their approaches and share feedback in relation to the effectiveness of collaborative learning. This supported the teachers to continually improve their practice and share best practice while being able to take risks within a safe and supportive environment.

Cognitive load

Cognitive load theory addresses techniques for managing working memory load in order to enable learners to process complex cognitive tasks (Paas et al., 2003). The aim is to reduce the load on the working memory so that it can function more efficiently. Teachers can reduce the load on the working memory by breaking down or 'chunking' information in manageable ways and by connecting new learning to previous learning. Research has also found that cognitive load in the classroom is exacerbated by adverse experiences to which students are exposed (Darling-Hammond et al., 2019). This is because the working memory is not only processing cognitive tasks; it is also processing emotional responses to situations that may be adversely impacting on the child. An example of this is a student who is experiencing bullying. Their working memory may be processing what they will do after the lesson to keep themselves safe as well as trying to process the subject content in the lesson. This results in overload to the working memory. It is therefore essential that teachers consider cognitive load and the limitations of working memory. Teachers must ensure that learning experiences are designed and delivered in a way which reduces the load on working memory. This supports learners to process information and move it into long-term memory so that it can be stored for retrieval at a later date. If teaching and learning activities overload a learner's working memory, then those activities will not directly contribute to learning.

CASE STUDY

A secondary school created several teaching and learning groups as part of its professional development programme. Each teaching and learning group consisted of teaching staff from across a range of subject areas. The groups were allowed to choose their own focus in relation to one aspect of teaching and learning. One of the groups decided to focus on the implications of cognitive load theory and working memory.

The teachers discussed their existing practice and together identified a list of strategies and approaches that could be used to support learners' working memory load. In summary, these strategies and approaches included:

- ensuring that lessons were tailored to learners' existing knowledge and skills;
- using worked examples to teach learners new knowledge, skills and concepts;
- incrementally increasing opportunities for independent problem-solving;
- removing inessential information or resequencing content;
- teaching complex knowledge and concepts by presenting them using a range of oral and visual techniques.

Teachers trialled these strategies and met regularly throughout the year to provide feedback. They also reviewed their curriculum plans to ensure that these strategies underpinned existing approaches to lesson planning.

Metacognition

Metacognition is the process of 'thinking about one's own thinking' (Georghiades, 2004). It facilitates a deeper conceptual understanding of content and more strategic learning. Students who have good metacognitive skills can effectively monitor their own learning, regulate their own behaviour, set themselves goals, monitor their own achievement towards these, and evaluate their own progress.

Research has found that students who employ metacognitive strategies, including self-regulated learning and goal-setting, are more able to engage in cognitive processes, remember information, and have greater capacity for learning (Farrington et al., 2012).

Teachers can model metacognitive strategies by modelling aloud their own thinking, particularly when they explain new subject content to students. Metacognitive abilities can also enhance motivation (Cantor et al., 2019) because students are aware of their own goals, strengths and weaknesses, and can evaluate their own learning in relation to their goals.

Students with good metacognitive skills can:

- reflect on their strengths and areas of growth;
- self-correct their errors;

- set their own goals;

- take ownership of their own learning;

- engage in regular revision and self-testing;

- act on feedback.

(Cantor et al., 2019)

Engagement and motivation

Learning is affected by motivation. Motivation is about the learner's perceptions of the task. A learning task will have more value to students if they perceive it to be important and relevant to their experiences and lives. Their willingness to apply effort is affected by whether they believe they will successfully accomplish the task (self-efficacy). Their motivation is also affected by their beliefs about intelligence and their capacity to improve their intellectual abilities. If they believe that their intelligence is fixed and they have no capacity to improve further, this can have a detrimental effect on their motivation. Motivation is likely to improve when effort and improvement are recognised and when mistakes are treated as learning opportunities rather than failures. The use of extrinsic rewards should be minimal and reduced over time. The belief that effort will lead to increased competence constitutes a growth mindset and results in greater achievement and wellbeing across academic, emotional and social domains (Dweck, 2017).

Executive functioning

Executive functioning is a term that is used to describe the processes of mental control and self-regulation. Therefore, executive functions involve the control and regulation of behaviours, including an individual's ability to control impulses, pay attention and remember information. Executive functioning skills are important as they help students to learn to organise themselves, plan their actions and think ahead. They enable individuals to make connections between prior and new learning and self-direct their own learning (Cantor et al., 2019). Teachers should ensure that their teaching is responsive to any skills deficiencies that learners may be facing. For example, if a learner speaks at inappropriate times and cannot regulate this impulse, then they must be explicitly taught the skill and behaviour of active listening.

What have you learned?

This chapter has introduced you to research about the brain. You have learned that neural plasticity and malleability enable the brain to continually adapt in response to experience. This means that direct experiences, including teaching, can have a significant impact on the structure of the brain. You have learned that each individual's development is non-linear and that developmentally positive relationships are critical to healthy brain development. You have learned about schemas, cognitive load theory and metacognition.

━━ FURTHER READING ━━

Baddeley, A., Eysenck, M.W. and Anderson, M.C. (2015) *Memory*, 2nd edn. London: Routledge.

Immordino-Yang, M.H. and Damasio, A. (2007) We feel, therefore we learn: the relevance of affective and social neuroscience to education. *Mind, Brain, and Education*, 1(1): 3–10.

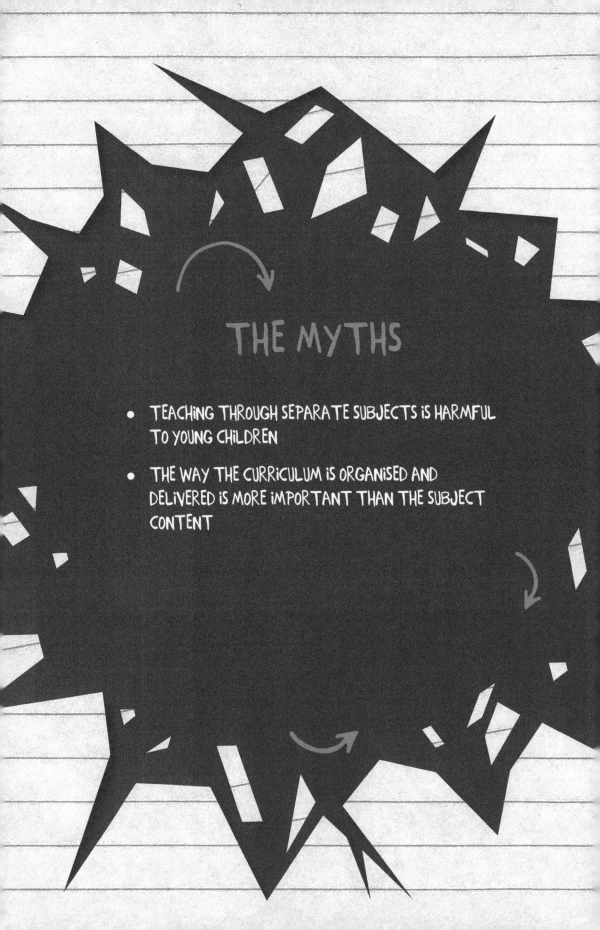

THE MYTHS

- TEACHING THROUGH SEPARATE SUBJECTS IS HARMFUL TO YOUNG CHILDREN

- THE WAY THE CURRICULUM IS ORGANISED AND DELIVERED IS MORE IMPORTANT THAN THE SUBJECT CONTENT

5

CURRICULUM ORGANISATION AND PLANNING

What will you learn?

This chapter introduces you to some key research into the principles of effective curriculum planning. It addresses aspects such as cultural capital, planning and sequencing the curriculum, curriculum breadth, and subject knowledge for teachers.

WHAT ARE THE MYTHS?

- Teaching through separate subjects is harmful to young children.
- The way the curriculum is organised and delivered is more important than the subject content.

Why should teachers challenge the myths?

Integrated approaches to curriculum planning have been popular in primary schools for many years. It is only in the last 20 years that schools have started to teach the core subjects (English, mathematics and science) separately. The foundation subjects (i.e. the humanities and arts subjects) are often taught through integrated approaches to curriculum planning. This has resulted in an insufficient focus on the subject-specific knowledge, concepts and skills that children need to know, understand and be able to do. The Education Inspection Framework (Ofsted, 2019) places the curriculum at the heart of a quality education. If children are not taught subject-specific content in the right order and at the right time, this makes the processes of assimilating and accommodating new learning difficult.

What do we mean by curriculum?

The curriculum stipulates what students will learn. It is designed to meet the needs of a society at a particular time, thus providing young people with the knowledge and skills that they will need in the future. According to Ofsted (2019), the curriculum:

is a framework for setting out the aims of a programme of education, including the knowledge and skills to be gained at each .... The curriculum lies at the heart of education. It determines what learners will know and be able to go on to do by the time they have finished that stage of their education.

(pp4–5)

There have been long-standing debates about how best to organise the school curriculum in relation to whether it should be organised into topics, themes or separate subjects. This chapter addresses these debates.

KEY RESEARCH

What is taught, how it is taught (Biesta, 2009), and who is included in the curriculum (Young, 2013) are key principles that underpin effective curriculum design. Research suggests that the humanities subjects have been marginalised from the primary curriculum (Barnes and Scoffham, 2017; Ofsted, 2002). In addition, research indicates that learners in receipt of pupil premium are less likely to take English Baccalaureate (EBacc) subjects compared with those not in receipt of pupil premium (Allen and Thompson, 2016).

International research demonstrates that curriculum narrowing is not specific to the UK. According to Berliner (2011), it has become commonplace across the US in response to the pressures of high-stakes testing. In Australia, evidence suggests that testing regimes have led to a reduction in the time spent on non-assessed subjects and impacted detrimentally on classroom pedagogy (Polesel et al., 2014) as a result of teaching to the test. Research suggests that teachers have been discouraged from experimenting with teaching strategies in the quest to improve test results (Ofsted, 2019).

Effective sequencing of the curriculum and use of retrieval practice helps learners to remember content. Research also suggests that repeating and reviewing key concepts (Scheerens and Bosker, 1997; Seidel and Shavelson, 2007) is a key characteristic of effective curriculum planning. As Sweller (2011) has pointed out, 'if nothing in the long-term memory has been altered, nothing has been learned' (p5). An effective approach to curriculum planning is to block learning and repeat practice over time, as this leads to better long-term retention of knowledge (Rawson and Kintsch, 2005). There is also increasing evidence that interleaving can improve long-term retention (Richland et al., 2005; Rohrer et al., 2015). Interleaving is the sequencing of learning tasks so that similar content or tasks are interspersed with different types of content or task rather than being consecutive. This results in a more variable and challenging learning experience but leads to better long-term retention. Retrieval practice strengthens memory and aids long-term retention (Barenberg et al., 2018; Roediger and Karpicke, 2006).

The research therefore suggests that regardless of the way in which the curriculum is organised, it should ensure that students grasp important subject-specific knowledge, concepts and skills.

Regardless of whether the curriculum is organised through subjects, topics or themes, it should be planned to enable learners to know, understand and remember key subject content. It should therefore activate neural networks in the brain that result in new ways of thinking and the development of new skills. It seems that the way in which the curriculum is sequenced is more important than whether a thematic or subject approach is adopted. The sequencing of knowledge and skills should enable students to make sense of what they have previously learned and support them in accommodating new knowledge.

Seminal work has highlighted that subjects are powerful tools for making sense of the world and that there is no danger in teaching primary school children through subjects (Alexander et al., 1992). In reality, many schools will continue to teach the curriculum using a combination of an integrated approach to curriculum planning and separate subject teaching. The problem is that integrated approaches to curriculum planning do not always ensure subject-specific knowledge and skills are covered in sufficient depth. In addition, poorly planned integrated approaches to curriculum planning can result in weak sequencing of knowledge and skills. If integrated approaches are adopted, the planning of the curriculum should ensure correct sequencing of the full range of knowledge and skills that students need to grasp within a subject. In addition, there should be regular opportunities for students to revisit subject-specific knowledge, concepts and skills.

Cultural capital

The Education Inspection Framework (Ofsted, 2019) emphasises the importance of schools developing a curriculum that provides students with cultural capital. Pierre Bourdieu (1986) was interested in how cultural capital is a source of inequality. Cultural capital has traditionally been associated with social class. The more cultural capital a person possesses, the greater chance they have of achieving social mobility. According to Bourdieu, cultural capital exists in three forms: embodied, objectified and institutional. An example of embodied cultural capital is accent. One's accent can restrict or support their chances of achieving social mobility. In addition, the more advanced one's vocabulary, the greater their chances of achieving social mobility. Objectified cultural capital is demonstrated through possessions because cultural capital can be exchanged for economic capital. People with greater cultural capital are more likely to live in bigger houses, wear designer clothes and purchase expensive cars. Institutional cultural capital is related to the type of school someone attends or their qualifications. Someone with a degree possesses more cultural capital than someone without a degree, and someone with a postgraduate degree holds more cultural capital than someone with an undergraduate degree. Someone who attends an independent school holds more cultural capital than someone who attends a state school. These forms of cultural capital can be exchanged for economic capital. Broadly, cultural capital is the accumulation of knowledge, attitudes and skills that enable an individual to demonstrate their cultural competence and social status. Cultural capital can therefore be demonstrated through social interests. For example, people with greater cultural capital may visit art galleries, museums, the opera and theatre.

So, how does this relate to the school curriculum? Given that cultural capital can be a major source of inequality, the curriculum should be designed to provide all learners with cultural capital so they can access future opportunities. There is no justifiable reason why people from working-class backgrounds cannot access high-status jobs. However, professions, including law and politics, are dominated by those from middle- and upper-class backgrounds. There is no justifiable reason why people from working-class backgrounds cannot access the top universities. The stark reality is that working-class people are significantly under-represented in high-status and high-earning professions and restricted from accessing the top universities. Sadly, discrimination and prejudice operate within our society; the capacity to purchase education provides greater future educational and employment opportunities, regardless of intelligence, and individuals continue to be judged on the basis of their accent, breadth of vocabulary and cultural experiences. Through embedding cultural capital in the curriculum, it is possible to increase learners' cultural capital by providing them with opportunities and experiences to which they would not normally gain access because of their social status and background. It is a way of providing all students with equality of opportunity so that learners from all backgrounds can achieve their full potential.

So, what are the implications for curriculum planning? One way of increasing learners' cultural capital is to develop their vocabulary. Increasing not only the number of words that learners know, understand and use in their communication, but also the complexity of the vocabulary, is one way of providing them with more cultural capital. Identify the complex vocabulary that relates to the subject matter that you are teaching and insist that learners use this vocabulary in both oral and written communication. Planning educational visits to places of interest is another way of developing cultural capital. Some learners may never have opportunities to leave their immediate locality. Visits to museums, historical sites, businesses, theatres and contrasting localities provide learners with rich experiences that broaden their interests and ambitions. Visits to local universities may provide learners with opportunities to be taught by leading experts within a subject and also raise their future aspirations. Bringing leading experts from the world of sport, business, the arts, sciences and humanities into the classroom to lead workshops can be aspirational for many young people. Bringing theatre groups, authors, poets, artists and designers into school can provide learners with opportunities to learn from people who make their livings within the professions.

The above suggestions are not exhaustive. They are intended to spark your thinking about how you can develop cultural capital within your subject area. Social deprivation does not have to be a barrier to success, but to succeed learners will require various forms of cultural capital so that they can perform when they write applications for university places and jobs and attend interviews. It is sad that people are judged on the basis of their cultural capital rather than their ability, but ensuring that all learners have the same opportunities for developing cultural capital is an attempt to level the playing field.

CASE STUDY

A secondary school leadership team asked subject leaders and the staff within their department to design a subject-based curriculum that provided students with cultural capital. Subject teams were asked to provide opportunities for developing students' cultural capital in each year group. Teachers were given opportunities to discuss and exchange their ideas so that each subject area understood the plans which were in place across the whole curriculum. This supported teachers to adapt and adopt ideas from other subject areas and to strengthen existing plans within their own curriculum area.

Planning and sequencing the curriculum

Effective planning and sequencing of the curriculum ensures that children learn subject-specific knowledge and skills in the right order. In primary schools, the starting point for planning is often the activities that children will undertake. Teachers are often assigned a topic or theme and they immediately start thinking of activities that children can do. The problem with this approach is that the knowledge and skills which children need to acquire often become an afterthought. The attention is often on the experiences with which children will be provided.

Although it is important to provide learners with a wide variety of stimulating experiences, it is essential to consider first and foremost what knowledge and skills you want the children to learn. What do you want them to know and be able to do by the end of this unit of work? There is little value in children making Roman mosaics and Roman shields if they do not know key facts about the Romans. These might include knowledge of the chronology related to that period, knowledge of the key events that occurred during the period, knowledge of the significant individuals who lived during that time, knowledge of important people and their lives, and knowledge of key vocabulary. So, the starting point for your planning needs to be focused on the knowledge and skills that you want your learners to develop.

You then need to decide how to sequence the knowledge and skills across a unit of work. Some teachers find it helpful to work backwards. If you know what you want your learners to know and be able to do by the end of the unit, you can then work backwards from this point to identify how the knowledge and skills will be sequentially ordered through the unit of work. Essentially, you will need to make decisions within a unit of work about what to teach first and the order of subsequent learning. You will need to consider carefully at the planning stage how the knowledge and skills will progress through the unit. It is important to share the bigger picture with your learners so that they know how each of the stages within a topic are supporting them to achieve a final goal.

If you know what the final outcome in a unit of work is, then you should be able to identify all the aspects of knowledge and skills (components) that will be required for learners to achieve this outcome. These components can then be taught throughout the unit of work and arranged in a logical sequence that enables learners to progressively develop their knowledge, skills and understanding.

A clearly and well-sequenced unit of work will support you in identifying the next steps in learning. This will enable you to provide specific students with additional levels of challenge, particularly more able students who can progress more quickly through the sequence of learning. A well-sequenced unit plan will also enable you to take the learning back a stage for learners who require additional consolidation.

Curriculum breadth

In recent years, there has been a narrowing of the curriculum, particularly in primary schools, where mathematics and English have been prioritised over other subjects. This has led to the marginalisation of the foundation subjects, and therefore lack of curriculum breadth. However, a broad curriculum in both primary and secondary schools (particularly in Years 7–9) is essential. Not only does a broad curriculum engage learners and support them in experiencing success in the subjects in which they are more confident, but it prepares them well for future employment.

Young people will need a wide variety of skills in the future for employment. They will need to be creative and adaptable and possess broad knowledge and skills. They will need to have good interpersonal skills, be able to work in teams, be resilient, and be able to solve problems. A broad and rich curriculum should provide children with all of these skills. It should motivate them, inspire them, and enable them to recognise their own strengths, talents and interests. Curriculum breadth promotes confidence and a positive sense of self. It maintains children's motivation and interest.

It is important that children have opportunities to study subjects in-depth rather than studying them superficially. An effective curriculum plan should enable learners to develop subject-specific knowledge and skills through high-quality teaching and opportunities for exploration and investigation.

In addition, schools should aim to develop curriculum breadth through a range of stimulating extracurricular activities. The extracurricular offer should provide opportunities for learners to specialise in a broad range of subjects. The introduction of a student debating society, for example, can provide learners with cultural capital.

CASE STUDY

A primary school developed an innovative curriculum plan to provide children with a variety of rich learning experiences. The curriculum plan provided the children with opportunities to learn about important themes, including climate change, mental health and politics. The time allocation for the humanities and arts subjects was increased and the school invested in a curriculum that fostered a sense of awe and wonder and created memories. To support their learning in geography, the school invested in educational visits to major national parks, towns and cities so that children could undertake geographical enquiries. The theme of climate change (particularly pollution) was addressed in a variety of geographical contexts. Children visited historical sites and participated in an archaeological dig.

Subject knowledge

Pedagogical content knowledge is consistently related to pupils' outcomes (Baumert et al., 2010; Wayne and Youngs, 2003). Baumert et al. (2010) found that teachers with greater content knowledge have higher levels of pedagogical content knowledge, which in itself leads to greater attention to cognitive activation in their teaching. Teachers therefore need to ensure that they understand the subject-specific knowledge, concepts and skills before they teach them.

NEXT STEPS

Examine the approach used in your school for curriculum planning. What subjects are taught separately? What subjects are taught using an integrated approach? How are subject-specific knowledge, concepts and skills sequenced? How does the school organise the curriculum to help students know, understand and remember key subject content?

What have you learned?

You have learned that some key principles underpin effective curriculum design and organisation regardless of whether the curriculum is taught through separate subjects or using an integrated approach. Subject-specific knowledge, concepts and skills are critical to students' understanding of subjects. Regardless of the approach adopted, schools should ensure that these are taught in the correct order to support students' understanding, and therefore teacher subject knowledge must be at the highest level. Curriculum breadth is important to ensure that students have access to a broad range of knowledge and skills. Opportunities to revisit and retrieve subject content are important. A curriculum that provides students with cultural capital ensures all students have equality of opportunity.

—— FURTHER READING ——

Department for Education (DfE) (2013) *The National Curriculum in England: Key Stages 1 and 2 Framework Document.* London: DfE.

Department for Education (DfE) (2014) *The National Curriculum in England: Key Stages 3 and 4 Framework Document.* London: DfE.

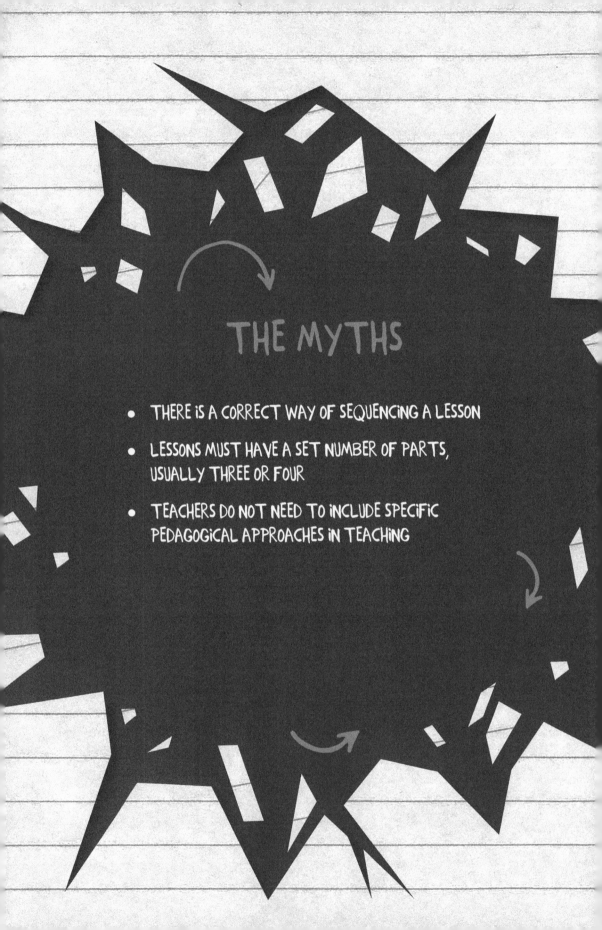

THE MYTHS

- THERE IS A CORRECT WAY OF SEQUENCING A LESSON

- LESSONS MUST HAVE A SET NUMBER OF PARTS, USUALLY THREE OR FOUR

- TEACHERS DO NOT NEED TO INCLUDE SPECIFIC PEDAGOGICAL APPROACHES IN TEACHING

6
PRiNCiPLES OF EFFECTiVE TEACHiNG

What will you learn?

This chapter outlines common myths in relation to the principles of effective teaching. Specifically, it addresses sequencing, planning and pedagogy. The chapter also outlines how national policies have reinforced these myths in recent years. In doing so, we support teachers to challenge these myths and we encourage you to reflect on your own practice within your context or setting. Key research is presented to demonstrate effective practice, and practical guidance is offered in relation to key areas of teaching and learning, including sequencing, assessment, modelling, scaffolding and questioning. Some case studies are provided to support you with a range of practical strategies and ideas.

WHAT ARE THE MYTHS?

- There is a correct way of sequencing a lesson.
- Lessons must have a set number of parts, usually three or four.
- Teachers do not need to include specific pedagogical approaches in teaching.

Why should teachers challenge the myths?

For many years, teachers have been trained to teach three- or four-part lessons that include distinct elements. Teachers have dutifully planned lessons that include starters, main activities and plenaries. National policies have encouraged teachers to plan lessons that include four or more timed elements. The worst example of this was the National Literacy Strategy, which was rolled out across primary schools in the late 1990s. These lessons were predictable and often safe, but rigid lesson structures have restricted teacher creativity. There is no single correct way of sequencing a lesson, and lessons do not have to include a specific number of parts. However, research has identified specific pedagogical approaches that are effective. This chapter outlines these, but it is important to emphasise from the start that these approaches do not need to be evident within a single lesson.

KEY RESEARCH

This section presents two models of effective teaching that are supported by empirical research. There are similarities between the models. The characteristics of effective teaching are then discussed further in the 'next steps' section. The important thing to note is that although both models identify the characteristics of effective teaching, the models do not specify that the principles should be implemented in a specific order throughout the duration of a lesson.

Rosenshine (2010, 2012) summarised ten principles of effective teaching:

1. Begin a lesson with a short review of previous learning.
2. Present new material in small steps, with student practice after each step.
3. Ask a large number of questions and check the responses of all students.
4. Provide models for problem-solving and worked examples.
5. Guide student practice.
6. Check for student understanding.
7. Obtain a high success rate.
8. Provide scaffolds for difficult tasks.
9. Require and monitor independent practice.
10. Engage students in weekly and monthly review.

Within this model, it is logical to start lessons by reviewing previous learning. However, questioning, modelling, student practice, scaffolding and checking for understanding may take place throughout the lesson rather than in a series of sequential steps. For example, a teacher may model new learning, then provide opportunities for guided and independent learning, then return to modelling to either address misconceptions or move on to more challenging subject content. The numbers within the model should not be interpreted as a sequential process. It is possible that a teacher may devote a single lesson to one aspect of this model rather than attempting to include all elements of the model within a single lesson.

Within the model suggested by Creemers and Kyriakides (2006) (see Table 1), some of the characteristics of effective teaching will logically follow a sequence. However, some characteristics, including questioning, modelling, application and assessment, may take place throughout the lesson. It is also possible that some lessons may be devoted to specific aspects of this model. For example, a lesson may completely focus on application tasks (5) or assessment (8). A single lesson does not therefore need to include all eight elements of the model. Therefore, the model is intended to provide a framework of the elements of effective teaching over time rather than within a single lesson.

Table 1   The dynamic model of educational effectiveness (adapted from Creemers and Kyriakides, 2006)

Characteristic	Effective strategies
(1) Orientation	(a) Providing the objectives for which a specific task/lesson/series of lessons take(s) place. (b) Challenging students to identify the reason why an activity is taking place in the lesson.
(2) Structuring	(a) Beginning with overviews and/or review of objectives. (b) Outlining the content to be covered and signalling transitions between lesson parts. (c) Drawing attention to and reviewing main ideas.
(3) Questioning	(a) Raising different types of questions (i.e. process and product) at appropriate difficulty level. (b) Giving time for students to respond. (c) Dealing with student responses.
(4) Teaching modelling	(a) Encouraging students to use problem-solving strategies presented by the teacher or other classmates. (b) Inviting students to develop strategies. (c) Promoting the idea of modelling.
(5) Application	(a) Using seatwork or small group tasks in order to provide needed practice and application opportunities. (b) Using application tasks as starting points for the next step of teaching and learning.
(6) The classroom as a learning environment	(a) Establishing on-task behaviour through the interactions they promote (i.e. teacher–student and student–student interactions). (b) Dealing with classroom disorder and student competition through establishing rules, persuading students to respect them, and using the rules.
(7) Management of time	(a) Organising the classroom environment. (b) Maximising engagement rates.
(8) Assessment	(a) Using appropriate techniques to collect data on student knowledge and skills. (b) Analysing data in order to identify student needs and report the results to students and parents. (c) Teachers evaluating their own practices.

Both models identify the characteristics of effective teaching. Each of these characteristics may not be present in a single lesson. They could be present across a unit of work. Therefore, it is completely acceptable for a teacher to spend a whole lesson modelling new learning if this is required. It is also acceptable for teachers to devote a whole lesson to student independent work if students require dedicated and uninterrupted time to focus on completing a task. However, the models do demonstrate that the principles of effective teaching should be embedded within a teacher's practice. Therefore, teaching cannot be deemed to be effective if it does not include specific pedagogical approaches such as assessment. This does not mean that specific characteristics need to be present in a single lesson, but they should be present throughout the duration of a sequence of lessons.

CASE STUDY

A team of subject teachers in a secondary school worked with a middle leader to discuss effective practice in relation to sequencing. The teachers deconstructed their existing curriculum plans and identified concepts and topics that must be taught and understood before learners would be able to understand more complex topics. The teachers also identified the skills that learners must possess before they are able to practise and develop subsequent skills. The teachers used this discussion to review the order and sequencing of their curriculum and to ensure that concepts, knowledge and skills were taught at the right time and in the right order. This supported learners' understanding and retention of the information they were being taught and ensured that they could retrieve key concepts and use their skills in unfamiliar contexts at a later date.

NEXT STEPS

This section discusses the key characteristics of effective teaching and identifies the implications for you as a teacher. These pedagogical approaches do not necessarily need to be evident in a single lesson.

Sequencing lessons

In the Education Inspection Framework (Ofsted, 2019), there is a significant focus on how effectively teachers sequence knowledge and skills within and across units of work. It is important when producing long-term and medium-term plans to consider how to organise knowledge and skills sequentially so that students are introduced to content in the right order and at the right time.

Reviewing previous learning

Reviewing previous learning is important because it enables you to check that students have understood what they have been taught. This enables you to ascertain if they are ready to move on to the next stage within their learning or whether they have developed misconceptions that need to be addressed. It is not adequate to simply ask students what they learned previously. You need to check that they have understood this subject content. The use of assessment tasks, questioning, tests and quizzes are helpful strategies for reviewing previous learning. Essentially, these should enable students to demonstrate their knowledge, understanding and skills.

Modelling

Modelling is an essential pedagogical approach when introducing new subject content. It may include specific approaches, including explaining and demonstrating new learning. These strategies may also be combined with questioning to develop students' thinking and check their understanding. Modelling enables you to demonstrate to students what is required of them. You can use modelling to demonstrate and explain a task or to demonstrate the expected standard that your students are expected to achieve. You can demonstrate a specific standard of work, concept, skill or strategy on the board or using a visualiser. The demonstration may be a visual demonstration of the subject content and could be used to supplement your verbal explanations.

Guided work

Students complete guided work usually before they complete independent work. After they have been introduced to new subject content, guided work provides students with an opportunity to develop their confidence with a specific task by gaining support from the teacher or from their peers. When students undertake guided work, they are not completely 'going solo' with a task. They might be working in pairs or small groups to complete a task before they complete a task independently. They might be completing a guided task independently as the teacher supports them to work through each of the required steps. They might be given the opportunity to instruct the teacher on how to complete a task so that you can check they have understood what is required before they complete the task independently. There are other ways of doing guided learning, but essentially this stepped approach to learning provides students with access to support prior to working independently.

Independent work

When students work independently, they are being given an opportunity to demonstrate what they know, understand and can do. Often students will continue to require support during independent work, and your role as a teacher is to monitor their learning, address misconceptions, provide them with frequent verbal and written feedback, and provide them with additional challenge if necessary. Students may sometimes need to spend a whole lesson or a series of lessons working independently. In the bad old days of the National Literacy Strategy, the time allocated for independent learning during lessons was minimal because the imposed lesson structure included too many different elements in the lesson, and this resulted in children not being given adequate time for extended independent writing.

Scaffolds

Teachers often model or demonstrate how to address a specific problem or concept. This allows them to offer support before stepping back and providing students with an opportunity to confront the problem or concept independently. This stepped approach ensures that the teacher is able to share their expertise while at the same time fostering students' independence.

It is worth considering the process of scaffolding as a continuum representing the actions and involvement of teachers and students:

1. modelling (teacher input);

2. guiding (mostly teacher input);

3. releasing (mostly student input);

4. independence (student input).

Some students benefit from a range of scaffolds to support them in completing tasks independently. However, it is important to ensure that scaffolding is used purposefully and meaningfully, not as a replacement to a learner's ability to develop independence. The scaffolds that teachers may use include:

*   writing frames;

*   vocabulary lists;

*   sentence starters;

*   worked examples;

*   describing concepts in different ways;

*   using visual aids;

*   activating prior knowledge;

*   connecting to background knowledge;

*   using a learner's first language;

*   reading aloud;

*   non-verbal gestures;

*   steps through a problem.

Use of assessment

The seminal work of Black and Wiliam (1998) has highlighted the important role that formative assessment plays in enhancing students' achievement. Effective assessment is integral to good teaching. It supports learners in understanding where they are now, where they are going, and how to get there.

Formative assessment is usually informal and low-stakes. Its use within and between lessons enables teachers to understand what stage students have reached in their learning and what they need to plan next. It informs teaching. It uses a broad range of strategies, including questioning, observation, marking and feedback, and tests and quizzes.

Effective formative assessment is used throughout a lesson rather than taking place at a specific stage of the lesson. It should be used at the start of the lesson to check knowledge, understanding and skills from previous learning. It should be used to check that students have understood the subject content prior to working independently on a task. In addition, it should be used during guided and independent learning to identify whether students have understood the subject content or whether they have developed misconceptions. Verbal feedback during lessons is particularly powerful, as is written feedback on students' work.

Assessment points should be integrated within units of work to check on students' understanding of the subject content over a series of lessons. In addition, an assessment point at the end of a unit of work will enable you to ascertain what students know, understand and can do at the end of a unit of work. It is also important to design retrieval tasks at specific points during the year to check that subject content has been transferred to students' long-term memories. Retrieval tasks can also be embedded within units of work to assess that subject content introduced much earlier in a unit of work has been retained.

Questioning

Questioning is another characteristic of effective teaching. It should be used frequently throughout lessons and units of work to check students' understanding. Effective questioning also promotes students' thinking by enabling them to reframe misconceptions and deepening their thinking. It is essential that high-quality questioning is seen as the cornerstone of effective pedagogy and planning, not as an afterthought or bolt-on. It is worth reflecting on your own approach to questioning to consider how you plan the questions that you ask. During this reflection, it may be helpful to ask yourself some key questions in relation to questioning:

- How often does your questioning require students to clarify their thinking rather than simply share their final answer with you? For example: *Can you tell me why you think that?*

- How does your questioning challenge students' assumptions? For example: *Do you think that is always the case? Why? Why not?*

- How often do you provide opportunities for students to think about why you are asking a particular question? For example: *Why do you think I asked you that specific question?*

- How does your questioning require students to think about the consequences or implications of their answer? For example: *If that was the case, then what else might be the case?*

- How does your questioning encourage students to consider alternative perspectives? For example: *How might you think about that in another way?*

CASE STUDY

The senior leadership of a secondary school dedicated existing teaching and learning time to the development of effective questioning strategies. The senior leaders decided to prioritise this aspect of teaching and learning following an audit of the school's strengths and areas for development. The teaching and learning time was initially used to provide teachers with an opportunity to discuss the characteristics of a good question. In summary, their responses included:

(Continued)

(Continued)

- thought-provoking;
- relevant;
- unambiguous;
- related to the objectives or criteria;
- clearly stated;
- properly directed;
- open-ended.

Subsequent teaching and learning time was used to provide teachers with a range of questioning strategies and to discuss how each could be applied within their own subject. The strategies that were discussed included:

- cold-calling (ensuring that learners remained alert and ready to be asked a question at any time);
- alternating between random selection and 'hands up';
- ensuring that adequate wait time was offered to enable learners to fully reflect;
- peppering (asking every student at least one question in every class);
- avoiding simplistic or closed questions.

Teachers were supported to trial a range of approaches in their own teaching and feed back their thoughts and feelings on each at regular points throughout the academic year. Subsequent teaching and learning audits found that the use of effective questioning had been strengthened throughout the school. Senior leaders continued to provide bespoke and tailored professional development to ensure that teaching staff joining the school were able to support this teaching and learning priority.

Learning behaviour

Clearly embedded rules and routines to support classroom behaviour will ensure that wasted learning time is minimised. Set clear expectations for student behaviour as they enter the classroom. Primary children do not enter a classroom at the beginning of every lesson. The focus for them has to be the transition between one lesson and the next. Providing a starter activity on the board for them to immediately engage with is a good way of settling them straight into work. Insist that they listen to you during the time you are directly addressing the class. Be prepared to stop and wait for them before you continue teaching and do not attempt to continue teaching if they are not listening. Reward positive behaviour and sanction poor behaviour in line with the school policy. Continually scan the class and address poor behaviour immediately. If necessary, speak to children individually and issue warnings. Ensure that you follow these through.

Develop clear expectations for independent working. Promote the characteristics of effective teaching and praise students who demonstrate these. These characteristics include:

- asking questions;

- persevering, especially with difficult tasks;

- effective listening;

- good collaboration skills;

- using specific strategies when they become 'stuck' in their learning, including making use of classroom-based resources to support them.

Managing a learner's misbehaviour does not necessarily support learning, but is likely to have an adverse impact on teacher wellbeing and workload. On the other hand, the explicit teaching of learning behaviours is crucial as it is likely to reduce the need for teachers to constantly manage misbehaviour. This is because these behaviours support learning and engagement through encouraging self-regulation (Ellis and Tod, 2018).

What have you learned?

This chapter has introduced you to some theoretical models of effective teaching. It has emphasised the importance of modelling in supporting students' understanding and the critical role that assessment plays in advancing learning within lessons.

—— FURTHER READING ——

Mead, D. (2019) *The Expert Teacher: Using Pedagogical Content Knowledge to Plan Superb Lessons.* Carmarthen: Independent Thinking Press.

Sherrington, T. (2019) *Rosenshine's Principles in Action.* Melton: John Catt Educational.

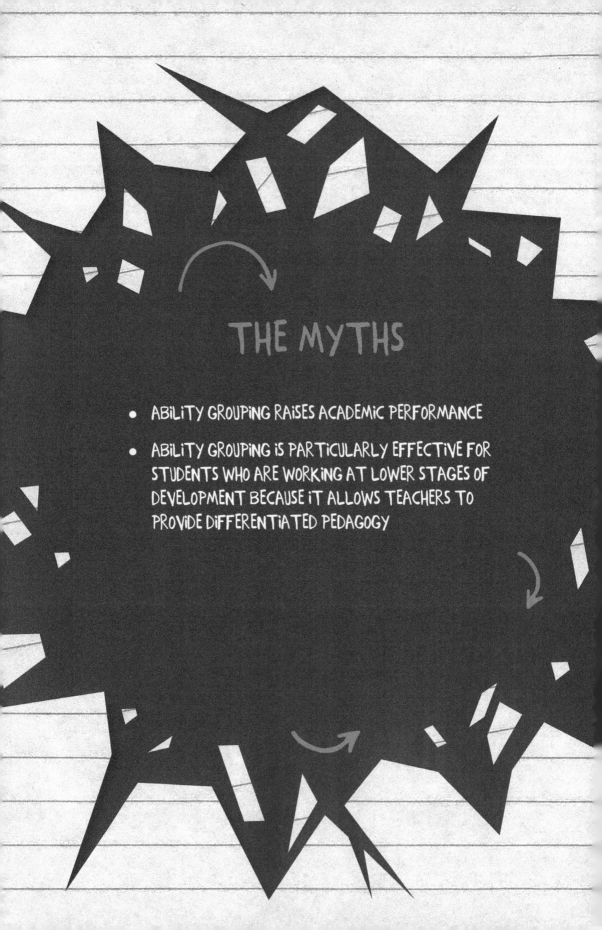

THE MYTHS

- ABILITY GROUPING RAISES ACADEMIC PERFORMANCE

- ABILITY GROUPING IS PARTICULARLY EFFECTIVE FOR STUDENTS WHO ARE WORKING AT LOWER STAGES OF DEVELOPMENT BECAUSE IT ALLOWS TEACHERS TO PROVIDE DIFFERENTIATED PEDAGOGY

7

GROUPING ARRANGEMENTS

What will you learn?

This chapter outlines myths in relation to ability grouping and highlights the importance of teachers addressing these myths through their professional practice. The chapter also introduces key research on grouping arrangements and identifies the implications of this research in relation to learners' progress and engagement. Additionally, some case study material is provided to exemplify effective practice.

WHAT ARE THE MYTHS?

- Ability grouping raises academic performance.
- Ability grouping is particularly effective for students who are working at lower stages of development because it allows teachers to provide differentiated pedagogy.

Why should teachers challenge the myths?

Within-class ability grouping is common in primary schools. Ability grouping takes various organisational forms in secondary schools, including setting or streaming. The research on grouping arrangements has been largely inconclusive. Some studies indicate positive effects on attainment and others suggest null effects (Slavin, 1987) or detrimental effects on the attainment of students who are assigned to lower-ability groups (Slavin, 1990). The problem with ability groups is that they can encourage a fixed mindset in both students and teachers. If teachers start to believe that some students are not very able, this can result in reduced expectations of them and assigning tasks which do not push them to the limits of their potential. In addition, ability grouping can place a ceiling on students' achievements because they may not be exposed to more challenging subject content.

Additionally, students in lower-ability groups can start to develop learned helplessness (Butkowsky and Willows, 1980) and they can disengage from learning and develop poor self-esteem (Felmlee and Eder, 1983). In contrast, students in mixed-ability groups tend to be exposed to the same subject content as other pupils, and therefore they are required to operate at the limits of their potential.

KEY RESEARCH

Hart et al. (2004) have demonstrated the negative effects of grouping students by attainment. These include reduced teacher expectations, undermining students' dignity and sense of hope, and access to a restricted curriculum for students in low-attainment groups. Slavin's (1987, 1990) research has demonstrated that ability grouping did not increase average student achievement, but impacted detrimentally on the achievement of students in lower-ability groups. Advocates of ability grouping emphasise the associated benefits of differentiated teaching and the importance of tailoring the curriculum and pedagogy to the needs of individual students (Tomlinson, 2000). However, research highlights the dangers of grouping and teaching students on the basis of achievement data, particularly for students in lower-attainment groups (Francis et al., 2017). It has been argued that assessment provides the 'quintessential vehicle for individualising and responsibilising success and failure' (Torrance, 2017, p83).

Research demonstrates that ability grouping can result in:

- misallocation of students to groups;
- a lack of fluidity in groups;
- poor-quality teaching for students in lower groups;
- differential pedagogy resulting in a widening of the achievement gap;
- reduced teacher expectations;
- negative student perceptions about themselves.

(Francis et al., 2017)

It has been argued that:

> Evidence on the effects of grouping by ability, either by allocating students to different classes, or to within-class groups, suggests that it makes very little difference to learning outcomes .... Although ability grouping can in theory allow teachers to target a narrower range of pace and content of lessons, it can also create an exaggerated sense of within-group homogeneity and between-group heterogeneity in the teacher's mind .... This can result in teachers failing to make necessary accommodations for the range of different needs within a supposedly homogeneous 'ability' group, and over-doing their accommodations for different groups, going too fast with the high-ability groups and too slow with the low.

(Coe et al., 2014, p23)

However, despite these concerns, it is important to consider that some research has demonstrated the positive effect of ability grouping on learners' progress and engagement (Francis et al., 2017). Ability grouping can support schools to individualise instruction through narrowing the range of ability and achievement within a class (Steenbergen-Hu et al., 2016). It has also been argued that ability grouping provides opportunities for learners to directly work with others whose ability and achievement are similar (Ireson, 1999). Furthermore, the teaching materials used within ability groupings are likely to be directly applicable to all pupils because of their similarity.

It is difficult to provide recommendations in relation to grouping arrangements as the research findings are inconclusive. Additionally, some research has failed to control variations in teacher quality between classes and groups. Nevertheless, it is still useful to reflect on existing arrangements and to consider whether mixed-ability grouping may be a suitable alternative to ability grouping. As research by Taylor et al. (2017) suggests a detrimental impact of setting by ability, it is clear that mixed-ability grouping may be a fairer approach. This is because mixed-ability grouping benefits the most and does not punish others to the extent that ability grouping does (Taylor et al., 2017).

CASE STUDY

A secondary school adopted mixed-ability grouping in Years 7-9 in all subjects. All students followed the same curriculum, which resulted in all students being exposed to the same subject content. In Years 9 and 10, students were split into ability groups for subjects that offered tiered examination papers. However, in some subjects that did not offer a tiered examination system (e.g. the humanities and arts subjects), students were taught in mixed-ability groups.

Teaching staff were given opportunities throughout the year to discuss the school's existing grouping arrangements. The school's leadership team supported teachers to understand existing research in relation to grouping arrangements and to reflect on existing practice. Teachers were also invited to share their feedback in relation to the effectiveness of different grouping arrangements. Senior leaders considered this feedback when making decisions about the curriculum provision. This ensured that grouping arrangements reflected the needs of learners and the subject area.

A case for flexible grouping

Within-class ability groups, setting or streaming are based on the assumption that students have a fixed ability across all aspects of a subject. A student might be a high-performing student within one subject, but it does not necessarily follow that the student will excel in all aspects of that subject. For example, a high-performing student in mathematics may be placed in the 'top' group but their proficiency in this subject may be based on their mental arithmetic. However, their skills in geometry may be less secure. If schools use ability groups, there may be a case for adopting a more flexible approach to grouping so that students can switch groups when different aspects of subject content are being taught. A student in the 'bottom' English group may struggle with reading and writing but they may have well-developed skills in spoken language. A student may be proficient in reading but not in writing. Keeping a student in a fixed group does not take account of the fact that abilities within a subject domain can vary. One of the fundamental problems with fixed-ability groups is that students are allocated to a group and they often stay in that group for the rest of the year, or even the rest of their time at the school. This does not take into account the fact that abilities can change over time.

CASE STUDY

A primary school decided to abandon ability groups for all lessons. Children sat at mixed-ability tables. During lessons, all pupils were exposed to the same challenging subject content. There was a significant focus on teacher modelling in all lessons. Teachers explicitly modelled the new learning using a variety of approaches. In some cases, this involved using the whiteboard or visualiser. Lessons were structured using the 'I, we, me' strategy. This worked as follows:

- *I*: The teacher modelled the subject content to the whole class. Modelling was repeated several times until the pupils understood the subject content.
- *We*: Pupils were given an opportunity to practise the new learning either in pairs or small groups. Sometimes during this stage of the lesson, the pupils guided the teacher by articulating the steps through the task.
- *Me*: Pupils worked independently on the subject content. Some pupils were provided with scaffolds to support them through the task. These included worked examples and steps to success, and some pupils had additional teacher input while working at their tables. The task was not differentiated, and there was a relentless focus on all pupils achieving the same learning outcomes.

NEXT STEPS

Consider the needs of the students in your class who are currently working at lower stages of development in specific subject content. Consider how you might ensure that these students make more rapid progress. Consider the benefits of 'pre-teaching' as a pedagogical approach. This ensures that students are able to work at the same level as their peers during lessons by pre-teaching specific knowledge and skills prior to the lesson.

What have you learned?

This chapter has introduced you to the advantages and disadvantages of different grouping arrangements. It has also introduced you to some key research findings into ability and mixed-ability groups. Through case studies, this chapter has illustrated some aspects of effective practice.

—— FURTHER READING ——————————————

Macqueen, S. (2012) Academic outcomes from between-class achievement grouping: the Australian primary context. *Australian Educational Researcher*, 39(1): 59–73.

Muijs, D. and Dunne, M. (2010) Setting by ability – or is it? A quantitative study of determinants of set placement in English secondary schools. *Educational Research*, 52(4): 391–407.

THE MYTHS

- DIFFERENTIATION IN CLASSROOMS IS NOT EFFECTIVE PRACTICE

8

DiFFERENTiATiON

What will you learn?

This chapter presents the research evidence on differentiation as a pedagogical approach. Differentiation is a strategy that teachers adopt to match teaching to the specific needs of individual students. This chapter argues that although this strategy now appears to be discredited in some educational frameworks and promoted in others, differentiation can be effective if it is implemented effectively.

WHAT ARE THE MYTHS?

- Differentiation in classrooms is not effective practice.

Why should teachers challenge the myths?

Terwel (2005) argues that differentiation has led to the emergence of inequality in classrooms. It has been suggested that the practice of differentiation in classrooms has been largely unsuccessful (Hertberg-Davis, 2009) and has restricted opportunities for learning for specific students (Taylor, 2017).

Although differentiation has been promoted as a pedagogical approach for at least three decades, the Education Inspection Framework states that teachers should 'adapt their teaching as necessary, without unnecessarily elaborate or differentiated approaches' (Ofsted, 2019, p9). It appears that the concept of differentiation no longer has credibility in schools despite the fact that the teachers' standards state teachers must 'know when and how to differentiate appropriately, using approaches which enable pupils to be taught effectively' (DfE, 2011, p11). However, while the Department for Education recommends differentiation as an important teaching and learning approach (DfE, 2011), no explicit guidance is offered on how this may be achieved (Taylor, 2017).

One of the key problems is that differentiation is difficult to do and is often done badly. As Taylor (2017) states, 'the notion of differentiation is often misunderstood and is regularly regarded by teachers as "scaffolding" for weaker learners and not as a framework for fulfilling the unique needs of all learners regardless of ability' (p58). Although the practice of differentiation is designed to address the individual needs of specific students, it has often been associated with setting, streaming and in-class ability grouping. These approaches have been addressed in Chapter 7, where it was argued that they can be detrimental to students' motivation and self-esteem, resulting in widening the ability gap. The research evidence presented in this chapter demonstrates that differentiation is an effective pedagogical tool when it is implemented effectively.

What is the problem with scaffolding?

Essentially, scaffolding is the support with which students are provided to help them move through their zone of proximal development. It can take a variety of forms, including resources, additional adult support, and guidance and questioning. Taylor (2017) indicates that this does not support differentiation, and there is some truth in this. If the scaffolding is never removed, then students will never achieve their full potential. Scaffolding should therefore be viewed as a temporary strategy to enable students to master subject content independently. An over-reliance on scaffolding can restrict students' independence in learning, and therefore restrict what they are capable of achieving. However, as a short-term strategy, scaffolding is an effective way of meeting the learning needs of individual students.

What is differentiation?

Differentiation recognises that learners are unique individuals with different educational profiles and needs. Through tailoring the teaching to the specific needs of learners, differentiation provides the opportunity for optimal learning (Petty, 2004). However, it is often associated with practices such as streaming, setting or in-class ability grouping (Terwel, 2005). Differentiation aims to encourage teachers to adapt their teaching, learning and assessment practice (Vickerman, 2009) rather than physically separating learners. These practices are adopted because they provide a convenient organisational strategy to targeting the needs of learners, despite the fact that they can result in widening the ability gap and damaging students' self-esteem and motivation (see Chapter 7).

According to Evans and Waring (2011), differentiation is not about providing different tasks; 'it is about creating challenge and supporting the learner in his/her development of strategies to cope in learning situations that are not always comfortable' (p152). Ensuring that all learners are appropriately challenged is critical, and differentiation should never be used to reduce the level of challenge to which a student is exposed. Sometimes it might be necessary to set specific learners different tasks, but this should not be the default position.

CASE STUDY

A teacher in a Year 3 class used a task board for specific children. She identified children who might struggle with specific mathematics tasks, and rather than differentiating by task, she used the task board to break the task down into a series of manageable steps with worked examples. She was keen that the children did not become too dependent on the task board, so she ensured it was only used when the children were starting to learn new subject content. As they developed greater mastery of the subject content, the children were expected to then work independently without the task board. This strategy of providing initial scaffolding, but then removing the scaffolding, ensured that children made similar progress to other pupils in the class.

The teacher adopted a similar strategy in English by providing specific children with sentence starters and writing frames to support their writing. However, they were only allowed to use these during the first few lessons of a unit. As children progressed through the unit, they were required to write with increasing independence.

KEY RESEARCH

Research demonstrates that effective use of differentiation can increase students' motivation and academic achievement and build on their previous knowledge (Konstantinou-Katzi et al., 2013; Munro, 2012). It is difficult to argue against the concept (Brighton et al., 2005) given its intended purpose. Research suggests that students benefit significantly when tasks are designed to match their individual learning needs (Brighton et al., 2005). Effective differentiation can fulfil the varied needs and abilities of students in the same classroom (Haelermans et al., 2015), negating the need for dividing students into sets and streams.

However, teachers' experiences and skills in adapting lessons to meet students' varied learning needs are paramount to the success of differentiation (Dixon et al., 2014). It is difficult to do well, time-consuming, and too often it results in specific groups of learners being assigned tasks that are not sufficiently challenging.

If differentiation is done well, the research cited here suggests that it can bring numerous benefits not only in securing academic gains, but also in producing motivational gains. It should therefore not be dismissed as an ineffective pedagogical approach.

CASE STUDY

A secondary school identified several students who struggled with literacy. They had not gained an official diagnosis of dyslexia, but they experienced significant difficulties in phonological processing, reading and writing. Their spelling was weak and their writing speed was slow. These difficulties caused significant barriers to their learning in lessons. They often had good ideas, but they could not express these quickly enough through their writing. They were slower than their peers at completing written tasks, and the focus on the technical skills of writing often meant that they did not have the mental capacity to think about the content of what they were writing.

The school addressed this problem by providing each of these students with a laptop so that they could use the word-processing software. This enabled them to pay more attention to the content of their writing than focusing on the technical skills of letter formation, spelling and sentence structure. They were able to use the software on the laptop to check spelling and grammar.

As a result of the technology, the students were able to work at the same pace as their peers.

NEXT STEPS

Practise experimenting with a range of differentiation strategies in your teaching. These may include:

- differentiated questioning that provides cognitive challenge;
- using peer teaching;
- extending the learning challenge;
- use of technology to remove barriers to learning;
- varying choices of task for students;
- offering students a range of challenges and asking them to select the level of challenge at which they wish to work;
- breaking down tasks further for specific students;
- use of additional resources to support learning.

What have you learned?

This chapter has introduced you to key research on differentiation. It has emphasised the importance of differentiation and outlined some strategies that you might adopt in your teaching.

FURTHER READING

Strand, S. (2010) Do some schools narrow the gap? Differential school effectiveness by ethnicity, gender, poverty, and prior achievement. *School Effectiveness and School Improvement*, 21(3): 289–314.

Westwood, P. (2013) *Inclusive and Adaptive Teaching*. London: Routledge.

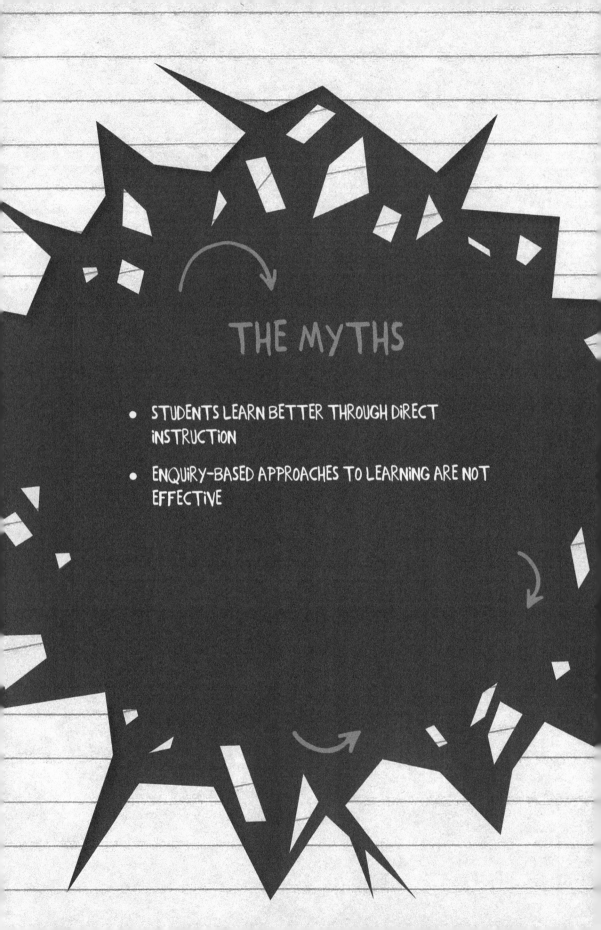

9
ACTIVE AND DISCOVERY LEARNING

What will you learn?

This chapter introduces you to some research findings on active and discovery learning. It emphasises that regardless of whether learning is active or passive, teaching must activate neural networks in the brain which facilitate new ways of thinking and new skills. It must enable students to connect knowledge with existing knowledge and it must facilitate conceptual understanding. The research on discovery learning is largely inconclusive, with some studies citing its benefits and others clearly stating that direct instruction is more effective.

WHAT ARE THE MYTHS?

- Students learn better through direct instruction.
- Enquiry-based approaches to learning are not effective.

Why should teachers challenge the myths?

Research published by the Sutton Trust (Coe et al., 2014) criticises discovery learning as a pedagogical approach. However, there are studies that suggest this approach may be effective. The Department for Education has produced guidance for early career teachers and teacher training institutions that clearly privileges direct instruction as a method of teaching. There is an emphasis within the Early Career Framework (DfE, 2019a) and the ITT Core Content Framework (DfE, 2019b) on explicit teacher instruction. Given that there is research evidence which supports enquiry-based learning and highlights academic gains for students, it is worrying that this pedagogical approach is dismissed within educational policies.

KEY RESEARCH

Memory is the residue of thought ... so if you want students to remember something you have to get them to think about it. This might be achieved by being 'active' or 'passive'.

(Coe et al., 2014, p24)

Students learn when they are actively thinking. This can occur through activities that are designed to provide students with first-hand experiences typically associated with 'learning by doing'. However, active thinking can also occur when students appear to be learning passively through traditional forms of direct instruction. The key point to emphasise is that learning occurs when students integrate new knowledge with existing knowledge, and this can occur through both of these pedagogical approaches. In fact, students may be learning nothing at all when they undertake an activity because the task is poorly designed. If the task is not pitched to provide cognitive challenge, then it is unlikely to lead to changes in thinking.

The following principles are necessary to promote learning:

- Teaching should build on and expand children's prior knowledge and experiences.
- Teaching should support conceptual understanding, engagement and motivation.
- Teaching should be designed to develop students' metacognitive capacity, agency and capacity for strategic learning.

(Darling-Hammond et al., 2019)

These principles can be achieved through experiential approaches to learning and transmission approaches. Cognitive science indicates that students learn more effectively when they are able to connect ideas from previous and new learning together. Well-designed tasks that provide learners with first-hand experiences can facilitate these connections, but so can more transitional modes of lesson delivery. Learning is enhanced when students create schemas for particular concepts into which they can place and connect what they are learning. Schemas enable students to form meaningful connections between ideas that provide coherence to domains of knowledge. In addition, cognitive scientists have found that organising knowledge in schemas facilitates retrieval and use of material from long-term memory. This was discussed in Chapter 4.

Learning should be engaging and challenging so that cognitive load is as high as possible. This can be achieved through experiential learning and more 'passive' approaches. Regardless of the mode of learning, it is critical that teaching supports the development of the three principles stated above.

A balance of experiential learning and more traditional didactic approaches is required to enable students to learn new subject content and to experience applying that content. The mastery of skills may require a more experiential approach to learning. Effective pedagogy is therefore not one approach or the other, but a combination of the two. As Cantor et al. (2019) have argued, 'there is no single "ideal" developmental pathway for everyone; instead there are multiple pathways to healthy development, learning, academic success, and resilience' (p9).

Building on prior knowledge and experiences

When learners integrate new knowledge with existing knowledge, this is when learning occurs. Students require repeated exposure to concepts to learn them. Students must make sense of new knowledge and accommodate this with their existing knowledge. Accommodating new knowledge within a framework of existing knowledge is not always a straightforward process, particularly when learners do not understand how the new content aligns with existing content that has been learned. Piaget (1975) used the term 'cognitive dissonance' within his writings to explain how this process can create a state of disequilibrium within the child.

Facilitating conceptual understanding

It has been argued that:

> *Direct instruction to provide information and develop a conceptual schema may be especially helpful when students are new to a topic or when they have entered a new domain through an enquiry-based approach and have developed key questions that motivate them to use new information that is now contextualized in their experience.*

> (Darling-Hammond et al., 2019, p21)

If students are learning through first-hand experiences, the teacher therefore plays a crucial role in facilitating students' conceptual understanding. Through explicit instruction, explanations, modelling and questioning, the skilled teacher can draw on students' practical learning experiences to develop their conceptual understanding. In this way, it is the role of the teacher to help students make meaningful connections between their prior knowledge and the new knowledge they have gained through the experience. Students do not automatically make that cognitive jump from what they already know to what they need to know. Thus, experiential learning provides students with a basis for developing conceptual understanding, but the teacher actively supports students to develop the conceptual understanding through direct, explicit instruction.

Discovery learning

Discovery learning is often referred to as enquiry-based learning, problem-based learning, collaborative learning or project-based learning. The research on discovery learning is inconclusive. This is a pedagogical approach where students discover knowledge for themselves, either individually or collaboratively.

According to Coe et al. (2014):

> *Enthusiasm for 'discovery learning' is not supported by research evidence, which broadly favours direct instruction …. Although learners do need to build new understanding on what they already know, if teachers want them to learn new ideas, knowledge or methods they need to teach them directly.*

> (p23)

Discovering things for themselves allows students to take an active role in knowledge construction to solve a problem or probe a question. Rather than receiving information and memorising it, discovery learning provokes active learning and student agency. Some research demonstrates that students exposed to this approach do as well as or better than their peers in standardised assessments, but significantly better on measures of higher-order thinking skills and problem-solving ability, and they demonstrate more positive attitudes towards learning (Barron and Darling-Hammond, 2008; Boaler, 2002; Bransford et al., 2004).

The EEF Teaching and Learning Toolkit states:

> *Over 40 years a number of systematic reviews and meta-analyses have provided consistent evidence about the benefits of collaborative learning .... Collaborative learning appears to work well for all ages if activities are suitably structured for learners' capabilities and positive evidence has been found across the curriculum.*

> (Higgins et al., 2014)

Discovery approaches to learning provide students with opportunities to learn to set goals, plan their work, and reflect on what they have learned and what more they need to know to solve a problem, overcome obstacles and communicate what they have found (Barron and Darling-Hammond, 2008). However, to be effective, students need defined learning goals, well-designed scaffolds, ongoing assessment, and access to resources to support information-gathering. The teacher plays a crucial role in supporting students to make sense of the knowledge that they discover, particularly in supporting them to accommodate the new knowledge within their existing schemas.

CASE STUDY

A primary school leadership team was concerned that teachers were resorting to explicit, direct teaching because it was less time-consuming to plan and resource. They were concerned about the concentration levels of very young children who were being expected to sit through long teacher expositions. The leadership team ran some training for staff on how to promote active engagement within teacher-led instruction. This process involved 'chunking' up the direct input by the teacher by interspersing teacher instruction with tasks that supported children to develop active thinking. Strategies for chunking included interleaving teacher exposition with short quizzes, tasks on whiteboards, paired talk, and asking students to demonstrate their learning on the whiteboard. Teachers were tasked with developing a broad range of tasks that they could integrate into whole-class teaching sessions. Children's engagement and motivation in lessons increased as a result of these changes.

Developing engagement and motivation

Regardless of whether learning is active, enquiry-based or facilitated through direct instruction, teachers need to expose students to content that motivates and engages them. All types of learning have the capacity to achieve this, providing that students perceive it to be interesting, important and relevant to their own experiences. Students' motivation is not only affected by the task content, but by their perceptions of their capacity to achieve a successful outcome. Students who believe that intelligence can be enhanced due to the plasticity of the brain are more likely to invest effort into tasks than students who believe that intelligence is static. It is therefore a worthwhile endeavour to develop within students a growth mindset.

Developing metacognitive capacity

Metacognition was considered in Chapter 4. Enquiry-based learning offers students greater opportunities for developing their metacognitive capabilities. This is because the tasks that are associated with this approach to learning usually require students to set goals, work in teams, plan their work, and monitor and evaluate their own learning. Metacognitive abilities are essential for long-term positive outcomes, and therefore it makes sense to include enquiry-based/discovery learning within the curriculum.

Developing agency

Enquiry-based learning provides agency to students because it gives them ownership of their learning. Through project-based learning, students often have to decide on a focus for the project, set goals, identify success criteria, and organise and plan their work to achieved specific outcomes by specific deadlines. These metacognitive skills are important for long-term development, but assigning ownership of these skills to students is likely to enhance their motivation.

CASE STUDY

A large secondary school had developed a mental health curriculum as part of a whole-school approach to mental health. The school was interested in enhancing the student partnership strand of the whole-school framework for mental health. Year 9 students were asked to research topics, and they worked in teams to research a variety of topics. These included social media and mental health, self-harm, anxiety and depression, the causes of mental ill health, resilience, vulnerable groups, and staying mentally healthy. Students planned a 15-minute presentation and designed a large poster for a display. The student presentations then formed the basis of a school mental health conference. Some groups made films, others designed a drama production, some groups did straightforward presentations, and one group designed a series of activities for delegates to participate in to support them in staying mentally healthy. Students contacted the local radio station and some students were interviewed live on air. Some groups carried out fieldwork to develop their research skills.

This project developed the students' metacognitive skills, including developing their capacities in planning, monitoring their own learning, evaluating their work, delegating tasks and goal-setting.

NEXT STEPS

Look carefully at your long-term plan to identify the subject content that you will be required to teach. Identify the pedagogical approaches that you will use to deliver the content. Identify opportunities for enquiry-based learning to develop the students' metacognitive capacities and to foster student motivation.

What have you learned?

This chapter has introduced you to some research findings on active and discovery learning. It has emphasised the important role of the teacher in supporting students to make connections between new learning and previous learning to facilitate conceptual understanding. The chapter has highlighted that the research on discovery learning is largely inconclusive and that a variety of pedagogical approaches can facilitate conceptual understanding. In addition, the chapter has highlighted the role of discovery learning in providing students with agency, developing motivation and developing students' executive functioning skills.

FURTHER READING

Brown, P.C., Roediger, H.L. and McDaniel, M.A. (2014) *Make It Stick: The Science of Successful Learning*. Cambridge, MA: Harvard University Press.

Willingham, D.T. (2008) What will improve a student's memory? *American Educator*, 32(4): 17–25.

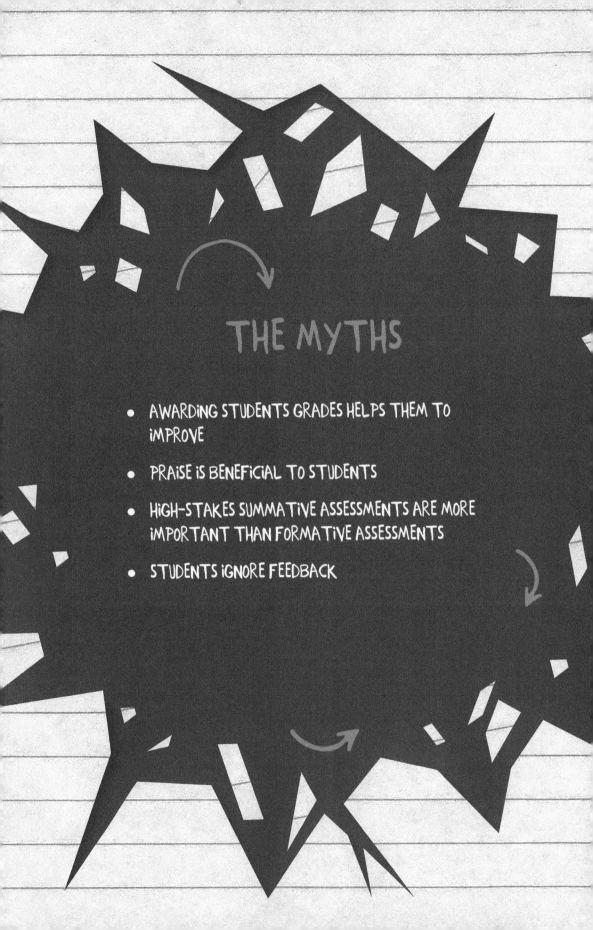

THE MYTHS

- AWARDING STUDENTS GRADES HELPS THEM TO IMPROVE

- PRAISE IS BENEFICIAL TO STUDENTS

- HIGH-STAKES SUMMATIVE ASSESSMENTS ARE MORE IMPORTANT THAN FORMATIVE ASSESSMENTS

- STUDENTS IGNORE FEEDBACK

10
ASSESSMENT

What will you learn?

This chapter addresses some common myths in relation to assessment and feedback. It identifies some of the seminal research in relation to this area and outlines some common approaches to formative assessment that you can use within your teaching. Case studies are used to exemplify ways of reducing teacher workload and embedding metacognitive assessment strategies into your teaching. This chapter emphasises the importance of combining assessment with teaching to maximise the impact of feedback on students' learning.

WHAT ARE THE MYTHS?

- Awarding students grades helps them to improve.
- Praise is beneficial to students.
- High-stakes summative assessments are more important than formative assessments.
- Students ignore feedback.

Why should teachers challenge the myths?

Assessment is a key professional skill for teachers. Teachers spend a great deal of time marking students' work and writing feedback for them to address. They also spend a significant amount of time creating assessment tasks and marking them. It is therefore important for teachers to know that these tasks actually have a positive impact on students' learning, given the time they invest in assessment.

However, assessment is not just about marking, grading and issuing feedback. Effective assessment takes place during lessons. It is usually informal and low-stakes, but evidence suggests that it has a significant impact on student learning (Black and Wiliam, 1998). There is no evidence that suggests providing students with detailed feedback on every piece of work is necessary to support their development. There is evidence that suggests awarding grades can detract students' attention away from written comments which are intended to support their development (Elliott et al., 2016), and there is evidence to demonstrate that specific feedback is helpful to students' learning (Elliott et al., 2016). In addition, evidence suggests that metacognitive self-assessment and combining feedback with teaching produce positive learning gains (Hattie and Timperley, 2007).

KEY RESEARCH

The key research findings in this area are summarised below:

- The majority of studies indicate that where grades are awarded on work alongside comments, students focus more on the grade and less on the comments. Students are therefore less likely to act on the comments to make further improvements. This reduces the impact of formative feedback.
- Feedback advances students' learning.
- The evidence suggests that providing students with generic praise, rather than specific praise, and praise which is not deserved when marking a piece of work is not beneficial. Praise may have negative consequences on students' self-evaluations of their ability, particularly if praise suggests to students that teachers have low expectations of what they can achieve (Hattie and Timperley, 2007).
- Research suggests that there is a strong case for providing dedicated time for students to consider and respond to feedback on marked work in class.
- Research suggests that the specificity of feedback is a key determinant of its impact on performance, while feedback that is imprecise may be viewed by pupils as useless or frustrating. Setting students clear, short-term targets is likely to have greater impact than longer-term targets.
- Research indicates that providing students with feedback on their work in the next lesson has a positive impact on student progress compared to slower feedback.

(Elliott et al., 2016)

In addition:

- Formative assessment leads to learning gains (Black and Wiliam, 1998).
- Metacognitive self-assessment promotes learning (Hattie and Timperley, 2007).
- Combining feedback with effective teaching in classrooms can promote learning gains (Hattie and Timperley, 2007).

Using the research to address the myths

Awarding students grades helps them to improve

From the research cited above, it would appear that the use of grades without formative feedback is unhelpful in promoting learning. The evidence also suggests that when grades are combined with feedback, they can detract students' attention away from the formative comments.

Praise is beneficial to students

The evidence cited above suggests that praise has to be specific and genuine. If praise is undeserved, students may interpret this to mean that the teacher has low expectations of them.

High-stakes summative assessments are more important than formative assessments

The seminal research by Black and Wiliam (1998) and Hattie and Timperley (2007) suggests that formative assessment plays a powerful role in raising achievement.

Students ignore feedback

The evidence suggests that students address feedback when they are given time in class to respond to it, when feedback is specific, and when students are set specific short-term targets rather than long-term targets.

What is formative assessment?

Black and Wiliam (1998) have defined formative assessment as 'all those activities undertaken by teachers, and/or their students to modify teaching and learning activities in which they [the students] are engaged' (p8). Black and Wiliam's seminal research into formative assessment has demonstrated that it plays a powerful role in advancing learning. Formative assessment is assessment that informs teaching. It enables students to understand where they are going, how they are going to get there and what they need to do next. It supports teachers in identifying what they need to do next to advance student achievement. Therefore, it informs planning and teaching. Unlike summative assessment, which provides a summary of a student's achievement over a period of time, formative assessment provides feedback to both teachers and learners. It helps teachers to ascertain if students have understood the subject matter and it enables them to identify and address misconceptions.

Using formative assessment in your lessons

Formative assessment takes a variety of forms. It often takes place during lessons to determine whether students have understood subject content that has been previously taught as well as new subject content that is introduced in the lesson. It enables teachers to identify and respond to misconceptions and to provide feedback to learners during and between lessons. It can also take place within and across units of work to ascertain whether knowledge and skills have been transferred to the long-term memory. The purpose of formative assessment is to provide both teachers and students with information about what students have achieved and where they need to go next. It is fundamentally not about grading or scoring student performance. It is usually informal and, unlike summative assessment, low-stakes in relation to school accountability. Approaches to formative assessment can include questioning, observations, marking and feedback, quizzes, tests, work scrutiny, and self- and peer assessment.

The importance of feedback

The research cited above demonstrates that feedback plays an important role in enhancing student learning. However, it is important that feedback is specific rather than general. Students need to know what aspects of their work are effective rather than being provided with vague generic feedback comments. In addition, the evidence cited in the research section demonstrates that the overuse of praise can be particularly detrimental to students, especially if students feel that praise is undeserved. Praise for students may be seen as positive, but research suggests that the wrong kinds of praise can be very harmful to learning (Hattie and Timperley, 2007). Students benefit from specific short-term targets. They also benefit from spending time within lessons addressing feedback comments.

It would appear that it is the quality of feedback rather than the amount of feedback which has an impact on student learning (Elliott et al., 2016). There is no need to mark every single piece of student work and provide extensive written comments. In addition, combining feedback with teaching is a particularly effective strategy, and this is captured in the following case studies.

CASE STUDY

A large secondary school decided to focus on providing students with verbal and written feedback during lessons to reduce teacher marking workload. During lessons, teachers moved around the students to provide feedback on their work. At the end of lessons, each teacher looked at a sample of student work to identify common misconceptions. They used this process to identify one key misconception that was then addressed in their teaching in the next lesson. Although they did not review all student work, teachers completed a 'deep mark' of each student's work every time the students completed a major independent piece of work. In addition, teachers modelled live marking using the visualiser during the lesson. They used this as an opportunity to model to students how to assess work. This was particularly effective during examination practice, when teachers used the visualiser to model responses to questions and then explained the allocation of marks to specific exam questions.

CASE STUDY

A primary school wanted to develop children's skills in self-assessment in writing. They encouraged the children to reread their writing after every paragraph and to consider the impact of it on the reader. The children reread the work and then made edits to it to include specific grammatical features that would create greater impact on the reader. They were provided with checklists to remind them of specific features to add, including adjectives, adverbs, similes and metaphors. This process of ongoing self-assessment was consistent across all classes in Key Stage 2. By the time the children reached Year 6, they no longer needed the checklist because they automatically knew the features they needed to add into their writing. The children used purple pens to make ongoing edits to their work.

Metacognitive strategies

Metacognition and self-regulation approaches have consistently high levels of impact, with pupils making an average of seven months' additional progress (Higgins et al., 2014). Metacognitive strategies help students think about their own learning more explicitly by teaching them specific strategies for planning, monitoring and evaluating their learning.

When students operate on this level, they are able to improve their own learning because they are continually self-assessing their learning and their work. They continually evaluate what they are doing to identify what they are doing well and what aspects they need to improve. They use this ongoing evaluation to make changes to their work to improve it as they go along. They are able to identify their mistakes and make corrections to these during the process of completing a piece of work rather than waiting to evaluate the final piece of work when it has been completed.

CASE STUDY

Subject departments in a secondary school provided students with questions from past examination papers. The students were asked to review the mark allocation for each question. After they had written an answer to each question, they were asked to self-assess it to identify whether their answer would achieve full marks. They were asked to add more to their answers if they had written an insufficient response to improve the quality of the answer. At the end of the activity, the teacher outlined the mark scheme for each answer and asked the students to allocate a mark to each question. The purpose of the strategy was to teach the students about the importance of continually monitoring and reviewing their written responses to questions to help them gauge whether they had written a quality response. This was a particularly effective strategy for questions that had large mark allocations.

NEXT STEPS

Consider the formative assessment strategies that you will use when planning units of work and lessons. The following points provide a helpful list of guidelines:

- Consider how you will assess students' knowledge and skills at the start of a unit of work (e.g. through a class mind map or an individual student self-assessment tool).

- Assess students' understanding of subject content that has been taught in previous lessons at the start of each new lesson.

- During lessons, use questioning to check understanding and promote thinking.

- Plan assessment tasks into your lessons to enable you to check if students have understood the subject content. These could include short quizzes and paired or group tasks.

- Circulate the room, noticing and addressing misconceptions. Provide students with verbal feedback and quick written feedback during lessons.

- Embed self- and peer assessment into your teaching. This does not have to be evident in every lesson.

- Consider when and how you will review the knowledge and skills that students have retained (e.g. midway through a unit of work, at the end of a unit of work, and six months after you have completed a unit of work). This will enable you to check that learning has transferred to the long-term memory.

- Combine feedback with teaching so that you use feedback to help students learn key subject content.

What have you learned?

This chapter has introduced you to some of the key research that underpins assessment. It has emphasised the need to assess students' learning during lessons through verbal and written feedback. It has explained how you might develop students' metacognitive skills in relation to self-assessment. It has outlined some of the characteristics of effective feedback. It has also provided a helpful checklist to remind you of the key things to remember.

FURTHER READING

Black, P. and Wiliam, D. (2009) Developing the theory of formative assessment. *Educational Assessment, Evaluation and Accountability*, 21(1): 5–31.

Christodoulou, D. (2017) *Making Good Progress: The Future of Assessment for Learning*. Oxford: Oxford University Press.

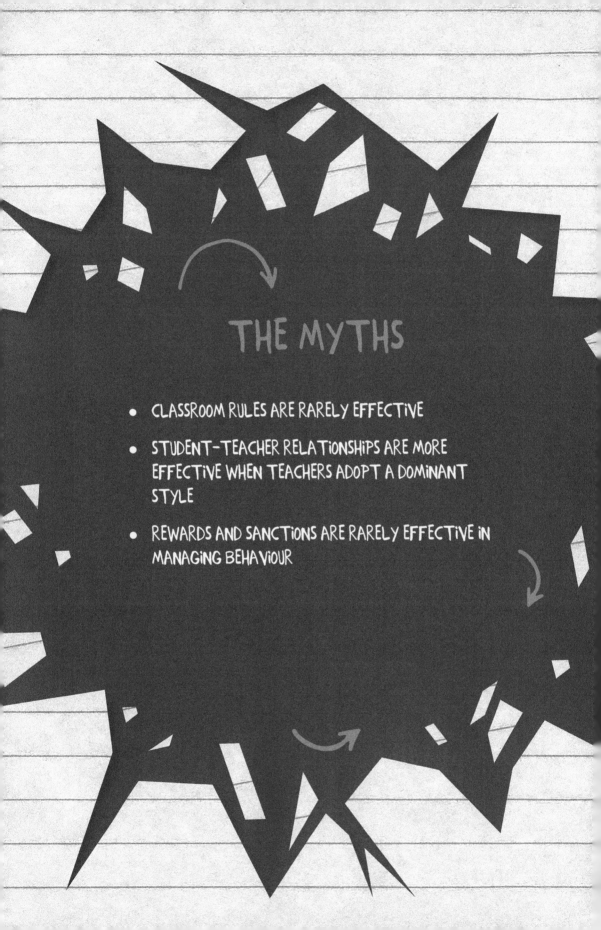

THE MYTHS

- CLASSROOM RULES ARE RARELY EFFECTIVE

- STUDENT-TEACHER RELATIONSHIPS ARE MORE EFFECTIVE WHEN TEACHERS ADOPT A DOMINANT STYLE

- REWARDS AND SANCTIONS ARE RARELY EFFECTIVE IN MANAGING BEHAVIOUR

11

BEHAViOUR MANAGEMENT

What will you learn?

This chapter presents some evidence-based strategies that you can use to support the management of student behaviour. Particular emphasis is given to the importance of rules and sanctions, teacher–student relationships, disciplinary interventions, and your mental mindset as a teacher. This chapter outlines some practical strategies for addressing common behaviour problems in the classroom.

WHAT ARE THE MYTHS?

- Classroom rules are rarely effective.
- Student-teacher relationships are more effective when teachers adopt a dominant style.
- Rewards and sanctions are rarely effective in managing behaviour.

Why should teachers challenge the myths?

Some 42 per cent of teachers who completed the Teacher Wellbeing Index 2019 (ESP, 2019) cited poor student behaviour as a cause of work-related stress. Poor student behaviour has a negative effect on teacher wellbeing, teacher retention and the progress of other students. There are a myriad of reasons to explain poor student behaviour. Although these have been well documented, there is less robust evidence about what strategies are effective in the classroom. At the same time, it is important to remember that specific approaches for managing student behaviour will vary in effectiveness between school contexts and between students in a single school. Research can pinpoint approaches that have been tested and have been proved to be effective, but this does not guarantee that you will find the silver bullet to solve all problems.

KEY RESEARCH

The research is drawn from a meta-analysis conducted by Marzano et al. (2003). This research summarises the findings of over 100 reports on behaviour management and 134 empirical studies. These studies were conducted with teachers within classroom contexts:

- The evidence cited in the meta-analysis demonstrates that classroom rules and routines have a significant effect on decreasing classroom disruptions.
- Strategies to improve the rapport and mutual respect between teachers and students also had a significant effect in decreasing classroom disruptions.
- The use of disciplinary interventions, including rewards and sanctions, show positive effects in minimising student disruption.
- The mental mindset of the teacher had the most significant effect in decreasing classroom disruptions.

(Marzano et al., 2003)

These findings challenge the myths that are stated above. This chapter will now explore each of these approaches to behaviour management.

Rules, expectations and procedures

Creating a positive, predictable and safe environment is essential in fostering positive student behaviour. It is important to create classroom rules and justify why these are necessary with the students. Rules should be phrased positively rather than negatively, but essentially they should communicate clear expectations of students' behaviour. Some teachers choose to involve students by negotiating rules with them in a bid to get them to 'buy into' them.

Establishing high expectations for behaviour will minimise disruption and maximise time for learning for everyone. You will need to work hard with classes initially to ensure that you consistently reinforce your expectations. High expectations may include the following:

- ensuring that learners enter the classroom in an orderly manner by greeting them at the door;
- ensuring that they start a task as soon as they enter the room by providing them with a task on the board;
- insisting that they work in silence at specific times when you ask them to work independently;
- ensuring that they are looking at you and listening to you when you are speaking to them ('Books closed, pens down, look this way');
- insisting that they persevere with tasks which they find difficult;
- establishing clear rules about movement around the room and sticking to a seating plan;
- setting clear expectations about participation in group work;

- being clear about how much work you expect them to complete in a specific time;

- managing transitions effectively as learners move from one activity to the next;

- establishing a reasonable working noise level;

- ensuring that learners attend lessons punctually;

- ensuring that learners bring the correct equipment with them to lessons.

CASE STUDY

A secondary school devised a questionnaire that was completed by staff, students and parents. The purpose of the questionnaire was to identify school and classroom rules that stakeholders considered to be important. The questionnaire asked the respondents to consider some pre-determined rules and assign each a score from 0 to 10 (0 = not important, 10 = very important). The results were collated and these data were analysed to identify the most important rules for classrooms and general school rules. This provided stakeholders with ownership of the rules, and parents and students appreciated being consulted.

Teacher–student relationships

Positive teacher–student relationships can result in students being more likely to agree to the rules and more willing to accept sanctions when they are issued (Petty, 2014). Relationships with students are influenced by your style. Some teachers adopt more dominant styles in the classroom whereas others are more collaborative. Dominant teachers tend to have a strong sense of purpose. They guide and control students and are prepared to implement sanctions unapologetically (Petty, 2014). However, teachers who are too dominant are too controlling, demonstrate a lack of concern for students, and do not establish good relationships with them (Petty, 2014). Teachers who are cooperative demonstrate great concern for the needs and opinions of students, are helpful and friendly, seek consensus, and avoid confrontation (Petty, 2014). Teachers who are too cooperative are often too understanding, too willing to accept student apologies, and often wait for students to demonstrate a readiness to learn. They often want to be liked by students (Petty, 2014). Research demonstrates that the most effective teachers tend to achieve a balance between dominance and cooperation (Marzano et al., 2003). They are not so dominant that they do not listen to students, but they are not so cooperative that they fail to lead.

You can establish greater dominance by adopting a confident posture and tone of voice. One good strategy is to keep moving around the room and to move closer to students, without invading their personal space, if they start to become disruptive. Maintaining eye contact is a useful strategy for expressing dominance, even if you have to hold eye contact for longer than you usually do. Students need to know that you have noticed them and you are not afraid of them. Use targeted questioning when you notice that they are not following the rules of the classroom. 'Why have you not started your work?' is more effective than 'Please get on with your work'.

Establish relationships with students by learning their names quickly and getting to know a bit about them personally. Notice them doing the right thing and issue praise where this is well-deserved. Petty (2014) refers to putting students in 'intensive care'. This process involves praising them, asking for their opinions, commenting favourably on their work, and demonstrating to them that you believe they can achieve and make the right behaviour choices. However, it is important to do this with all students, not just those who demonstrate problematic behaviour.

Simple and effective ways of establishing relationships with new classes include the following:

- learn the names of all learners very quickly (a seating plan will help with this);
- smile;
- try to get to know your learners, including their interests outside of school;
- thank them for their contributions in class;
- acknowledge the effort they make with their work;
- create a 'can-do' culture so that learners start to believe in their abilities;
- apologise to learners if you make a mistake;
- tell them a little about yourself;
- be enthusiastic about your teaching (if you are excited, it will be infectious);
- use eye contact;
- use their names in class.

Disciplinary interventions

Marzano et al. (2003) found that a combination of mild sanctions and rewards for appropriate behaviour has a greater effect size in reducing the number of disruptions than the use of sanctions on their own. Rewards may include:

- positive letters sent to parents and carers;
- privileges;
- certificates;
- stickers, points or smiley faces.

Sanctions should be used when students break the rules, but consistency of approach is more important than the severity of the sanction (Marzano et al., 2003). Be decisive when implementing sanctions so that students comply with your command (e.g. if you ask a student to move seats). If the student does not comply, issue a warning that non-compliance will lead to serious consequences, terminate the conversation, and move away from them. Ensure that you follow this up after the lesson.

CASE STUDY

A primary school developed a praise blog for each classroom. At the end of each day, each teacher nominated specific pupils to be acknowledged on the blog for effort, achievement or character. Their names were listed on the blog and this was supplemented with the reason for the nomination. In addition, praise was also communicated to parents via emails, text messages or phone calls, depending on the parents' preferred method of communication.

Mental set

Mental set includes:

- *'Withitness'*: This is about being very aware of what is going on in the classroom and addressing poor behaviour immediately before it has a chance to escalate.

- *Emotional objectivity*: This involves not taking behaviour personally and being prepared to 'wipe the slate clean' after an incident has been addressed.

Research demonstrates that both of these strategies have a significant effect on decreasing the number of classroom disruptions (Marzano et al., 2003).

'Withitness' strategies include:

- scanning the class from the edges of the classroom;

- using eye contact and intervening promptly, if necessary, by moving close to students;

- using students' names;

- stopping teaching the moment a student starts talking or behaving inappropriately, then making eye contact with the student;

- using non-verbal cues to address disruption;

- creating smooth transitions (e.g. moving one group at a time or having resources ready on tables);

- walking around the room, making effective use of eye contact.

(Petty, 2014)

Promoting positive learning behaviour

In recent years, there has been a move away from the term 'behaviour management' to 'behaviour for learning', despite the former term being adopted in the teachers' standards (DfE, 2011). Learners demonstrate good learning behaviour when they are:

- listening;

- collaborating;

- asking questions;

- challenging other people's opinions about subject content;

- persevering when they find something difficult;

- managing distractions;

- making connections between different aspects of learning;

- noticing;

- being independent;

- using tools for learning when they become 'stuck' rather than depending on a teacher.

Some learners find it difficult to participate in lessons. They do not ask questions and they tend to be passive. Quiet, passive and compliant behaviour is not good learning behaviour. You need to encourage your learners to ask questions, to affirm other people's responses, or to challenge them, and to keep trying when they are working on a really difficult problem. Effective learners manage their distractions well. If there is disruption taking place, or if someone walks into the room to talk to you, effective learners manage these distractions well and continue with their task. Some learners waste valuable learning time when they become 'stuck' in their learning. This stops them from making progress in the lesson. Through teaching the students a four-step process, you can offer them a framework to guide their response when this happens. When learners become 'stuck', you can encourage them to:

1. **T**hink.

2. **T**alk to a peer.

3. Use **T**ools for learning (resources to help them with their learning).

4. Talk to a **Te**acher.

The 4Ts approach ensures that the last thing they do if they become stuck is to ask a teacher. When you see learners demonstrating good learning behaviours, you should provide positive descriptive praise (e.g. 'I liked the way you persevered with that task', 'I saw some really great collaboration in that group').

NEXT STEPS

Review your school behaviour policy to identify the strategies you are required to implement in your lessons. Identify if there is scope for developing your own strategies in addition to those set out in the policy. Discuss with colleagues which aspects of managing behaviour you find more difficult and which classes or pupils you find more challenging. Talk through these situations with supportive colleagues and ask for practical advice.

What have you learned?

This chapter has emphasised the importance of establishing rules, expectations and procedures to support the management of student behaviour. It has stressed the importance of teacher–student relations, in particular the importance of developing an optimal balance between cooperation and dominance. It has outlined the need to use a combination of rewards and sanctions in your teaching. Finally, it has stressed the need for you to have conscious control over your thoughts and feelings when you respond to specific situations, and not to view negative behaviour as a personal attack on you.

 **FURTHER READING**

Cowley, S. (2014) *Getting the Buggers to Behave*. London: Bloomsbury.

Mortimer, H. (2017) *Understanding Behaviour in Early Years Settings*. London: David Fulton Publishers.

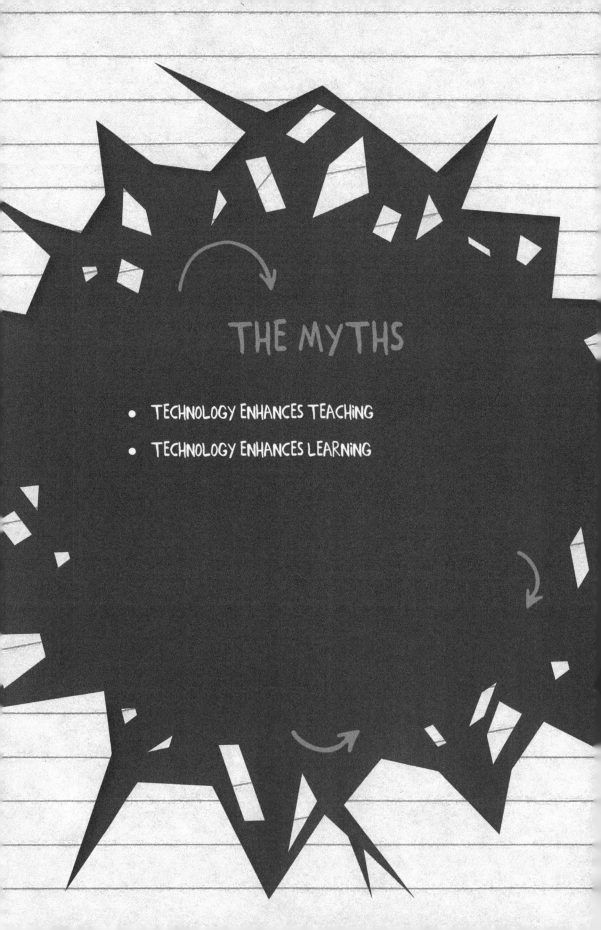

12

USING TECHNOLOGY

What will you learn?

This chapter presents some of the research into the use of technology in teaching and learning, drawing on evidence from the Education Endowment Foundation (EEF). It will explore the potential benefits and limitations of using technology in schools. Through case studies, it will illustrate specific pedagogical approaches, including flipped learning and the use of technology to support formative assessment.

WHAT ARE THE MYTHS?

- Technology enhances teaching.
- Technology enhances learning.

Why should teachers challenge the myths?

Educators are interested in pedagogical approaches that promote student engagement (Britt, 2014; Lee and Hannafin, 2016). Technology has become embedded throughout society, and schools are therefore expected to use technology to enhance teaching and learning. Technology in schools can take a variety of forms. These include:

- technology for students, where learners use programs or applications designed for problem-solving or open-ended learning;

- technology for teachers, including interactive whiteboards or learning platforms.

However, the assumption that using technology enhances learning is not always accurate. This chapter will explore the benefits of using technology to enhance learning and teaching, and the associated issues.

CASE STUDY

A secondary school psychology department decided to experiment with flipped learning. The teachers made a series of ten-minute videos to explain different psychological theories. The homework was for the students to view one specific video before attending the lesson. In the lesson, the starter activity was a short quiz on paper to check which students had engaged with the subject content and to identify those that had not. This was marked during the lesson. The teacher then asked several quick questions to check the students' understanding of the theory. The rest of the lesson was then devoted to practical experiments or analysis of case studies. Students were required to demonstrate their understanding of the psychological theory through the analysis of case studies or they conducted experiments to test the theory. This approach gave the students ownership of their learning and it meant more time could be spent in the lesson on developing students' application of the theory. The software allowed the teacher to identify which students had viewed the video prior to the lesson.

KEY RESEARCH

According to the latest report by the Education Endowment Foundation, *Using Digital Technology to Improve Learning* (Stringer et al., 2019), technology is most effective when it is used to supplement or enhance teaching rather than replace it. The key points addressed in this report are summarised below:

- Technology can enhance teacher explanations and modelling in lessons.
- Simulations and virtual experiments in science subjects should supplement practical scientific investigations rather than replacing them.
- Technology can increase student motivation, but motivation does not necessarily result in learning.
- Where students do not have the skills to use technology, this can widen the ability gap rather than narrowing it.
- Technology can be used to support assessment and feedback. However, if teachers do not use the assessment data to improve their teaching, and if students do not act on the feedback, this does not necessarily result in learning. Therefore, the important point is not the use of the technology per se, but what teachers and students do with the information that the technology generates. This is what promotes learning. The report states that:

Technology has the potential to improve both assessment and feedback, particularly in terms of speed and efficiency. However, as with other aspects of teaching, the degree to which this potential is realised will be determined by pedagogy and implementation. In particular, how teachers use information from assessments, and how pupils act on feedback, matter more than the way in which they are collected and delivered.

(Stringer et al., 2019, p20)

- Teachers need to have a clear rationale for using technology. Technology serves no purpose if an alternative pedagogical approach could be adopted that is more effective.
- Evidence suggests that teachers can use technology to increase the benefits of practice to improve fluency or retention of information, and that this is likely to have a positive impact on learning (Cheung and Slavin, 2013).
- The effectiveness of technology will ultimately be determined by the quality of the pedagogy underpinning a program's design and the way in which it is implemented (Belland et al., 2016).

The research findings suggest that although the use of technology can be beneficial in enhancing learning and teaching, this is not automatic, and it depends on various factors. These include the effectiveness of the technology in promoting learning rather than just motivation, how well students and teachers use the information generated by the technology, and whether there is a clear pedagogic rationale for using the technology.

In the worst-case scenario, technology is used to replace students' access to rich first-hand experiences. Virtual science experiments should not replace the opportunity for students to undertake scientific investigations. In early years classrooms, displays of mathematical shapes on an interactive whiteboard should never replace the opportunity for children to handle shapes. Electronic books should not replace children's exposure to physical books. Presentational software should not replace opportunities for students to explore, investigate and learn through their senses. These are examples of where technology might be used to complement traditional pedagogical approaches, but to replace first-hand experiences with technology would be restricting opportunities for deep, rich, experiential learning. Technology can support teachers with modelling, but in some instances modelling is more effective by showing children manipulative resources. The need for teachers to have a clear rationale for using technology as a pedagogical tool therefore cannot be overstated.

CASE STUDY

A primary school developed a series of online quizzes to assess children's understanding of subject content that had been taught. Each quiz focused on a specific aspect of subject content and was released to the children after the lesson. The homework task was for students to complete the quiz. The children had to select the appropriate answer to a question from a set of answers. Once they submitted their answers, they received immediate feedback and a score. The teacher could also view the scores. If children gained a low score, the software provided them with written feedback based on the analysis of their responses to the questions. They could retake the quiz multiple times, and the teacher was able to view the number of attempts and their scores. This approach was effective because the children gained instant feedback, they were motivated to complete the assessments, and the teacher did not have to mark the homework!

─────── NEXT STEPS ───────

Review the units of work that you are responsible for teaching on your long-term plan and consider how the use of technology might enhance teaching and learning in specific lessons.

What have you learned?

This chapter has introduced you to the EEF research into the role of technology in teaching and learning. It has emphasised the need to have a clear rationale for the use of technology. It has also stressed the importance of using technology to enhance learning but not to replace more effective pedagogical approaches with technology. In some cases, technology will enhance learning. In others, it will restrict learning. This chapter has provided two examples through case studies of how to use technology to enhance assessment and feedback. However, it has also emphasised the need for both teachers and students to use the data that are generated by the software to enhance learning.

── FURTHER READING ─────────────────────────

Higgins, S. (2010) The impact of interactive whiteboards on classroom interaction and learning in primary schools in the UK. In M. Thomas and E.C. Schmid (eds), *Interactive Whiteboards for Education: Theory, Research and Practice*. Hershey, PA: IGI Global.

Wouters, P., van Nimwegen, C., van Oostendorp, H. and van der Spek, E.D. (2013) A meta-analysis of the cognitive and motivational effects of serious games. *Journal of Educational Psychology*, 105(2): 249–65.

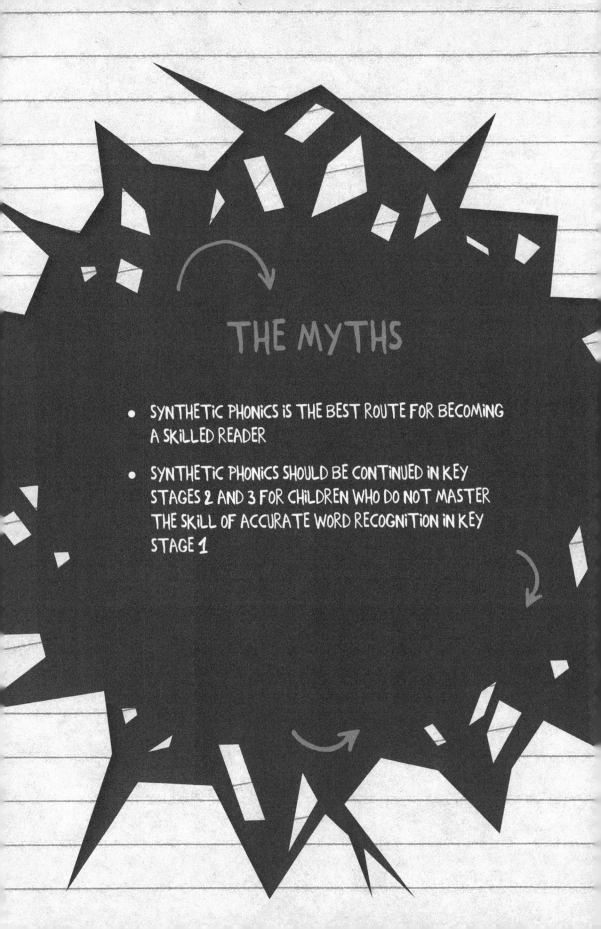

THE MYTHS

- SYNTHETIC PHONICS IS THE BEST ROUTE FOR BECOMING A SKILLED READER

- SYNTHETIC PHONICS SHOULD BE CONTINUED IN KEY STAGES 2 AND 3 FOR CHILDREN WHO DO NOT MASTER THE SKILL OF ACCURATE WORD RECOGNITION IN KEY STAGE 1

13
SYNTHETIC PHONICS

What will you learn?

This chapter introduces key research in relation to synthetic phonics. In doing so, it emphasises the importance of schools providing children with a programme of systematic synthetic phonics instruction. The chapter outlines key myths in relation to the teaching of phonics and highlights the need for teachers to challenge these through their professional practice. Practical guidance is offered to support your teaching of phonics, and the chapter provides some consideration of phonics teaching in relation to the national and international context. Additionally, the chapter discusses the development of phonological and phonemic awareness, and the implications of these are outlined in relation to the delivery of phonics programmes. Some case study material is also provided to illuminate effective practice and encourage you to reflect on your existing provision.

WHAT ARE THE MYTHS?

- Synthetic phonics is the best route for becoming a skilled reader.
- Synthetic phonics should be continued in Key Stages 2 and 3 for children who do not master the skill of accurate word recognition in Key Stage 1.

Policy context

Following the publication of the *Independent Review of the Teaching of Early Reading* by Jim Rose (DfES, 2006), educational policy in England has continued to emphasise the need for schools to provide children with a programme of systematic synthetic phonics instruction. The Rose Review concluded that 'the case for systematic phonic work is overwhelming and much strengthened by a synthetic approach' (DfES, 2006, p20). In this review, Rose recommended that synthetic phonics 'offers the best route to becoming skilled readers' (p19). Following this significant recommendation, schools across England were required by local authorities and inspectors to adopt synthetic phonics as the preferred approach for teaching reading. In addition, inspections of initial teacher training courses focused extensively on the depth of trainees' subject knowledge and their practical experiences of observing and teaching synthetic phonics. The emphasis on synthetic phonics was subsequently embedded in the teachers' standards (DfE, 2011), and the Year 1 phonics screening check was introduced in 2012 to ensure that the skill of decoding is secure before children progress into Year 2. The emphasis on synthetic phonics became a political priority for the New Labour government in 2006. Successive governments have continued this policy priority despite abandoning most other education policies from previous governments. Synthetic phonics has therefore stood the test of time.

Why should teachers challenge the myths?

Adopting synthetic phonics as a 'one-size-fits-all' approach to early reading development has been appropriate for many children but certainly not for all children. However, teachers have been systematically de-professionalised. Synthetic phonics has become hugely political. The government continues to believe that it provides the 'silver bullet' for addressing the significant trail of underachievement in reading which has existed in England for many decades. The stark reality is that in 2019, only 73 per cent of pupils in Key Stage 2 reached the expected standard in reading, and there is currently a downward trend in attainment (DfE, 2019c). Girls continue to outperform boys at the expected standard across all subjects that are tested (DfE, 2019c). The latest PIRLS data from 2016 (DfE, 2017) demonstrate that one-fifth of pupils in England reported that they did not enjoy reading. In view of these statistics, it might be argued that synthetic phonics is not the silver bullet it was intended to be. Given that over one-quarter of children are currently not reading at an age-appropriate level at the end of Key Stage 2, and that there are variations in reading attainment between boys and girls, it is justifiable to make the case that that one size does not fit all.

KEY RESEARCH

The term 'synthetic' is taken from the verb 'to synthesise'. Beginning readers are taught grapheme-phoneme correspondences and taught to blend phonemes (sounds) all through the word right from the outset in order to develop word reading skills (Johnston and Watson, 2007). They are also taught the reverse process of segmenting a spoken word into its constituent phonemes. These are then represented as graphemes for spelling. In synthetic phonics, words are broken down into the smallest meaningful units of sound (e.g. b-oa-t or th-r-oa-t). In contrast, in analytic phonics, words are broken down into onset and rimes (e.g. b-oat or thr-oat).

Rose drew evidence from the Clackmannanshire research in Scotland (Watson and Johnston, 1998). The research examined the performance of three groups of children who received intervention over a ten-week period. One group received sight vocabulary training, a second group received intervention in analytic phonics, and a third group received intervention in synthetic phonics. The results led the researchers to conclude that synthetic phonics led to better reading, spelling and phonemic awareness gains than the other two approaches (Watson and Johnston, 1998).

However, the Clackmannanshire research has received considerable criticism in the academic litera-ture (Wyse and Goswami, 2008). The study lacked sufficient rigour in its design to establish whether the synthetic approach was superior to the analytic approach (Wyse and Goswami, 2008). Children in the analytic phonics group were taught fewer letters than children in the synthetic phonics group and the groups were given different amounts of teaching (Wyse and Styles, 2007). Additionally, the research design did not isolate the impact of additional treatment factors (or confounds), which might have contributed to the gains in reading, spelling and phonemic awareness for those children in the synthetic phonics group (Ellis and Moss, 2014). For example, factors such as teacher effective-ness, parents' educational attainment, the quality of the literacy environment in the home, reme-dial help offered outside the intervention, and other reading interventions that operated within the school were not controlled, and therefore the evidence is insufficiently robust (Ellis and Moss, 2014). The study failed to report information about time spent on phonics instruction outside the inter-vention, time spent on other reading activities, and the contexts in which children were exposed to phonics (Ellis and Moss, 2014). Given these serious flaws in the reporting of the research and the design of the study, Ellis and Moss (2014) have concluded that 'the weakness of the research design, including the way the statistical data were analysed and reported, suggests it would be unwise to draw any clear conclusions for pedagogy or policy from this single study' (p249). Research by Price-Mohr and Price (2018) with a group of underachieving readers aged 5-6 years demonstrates that a variety of approaches, including sight word vocabulary, oral vocabulary extension and analytic phonics, produced positive benefits in addition to synthetic phonics. In addition, they found that exposure to non-decodable words in reading books was also helpful in promoting reading development.

According to Torgerson et al. (2006), 'there is currently no strong randomised controlled trial evi-dence that any one form of systematic phonics is more effective than any other' (p49). Research evidence that is available is insufficient to allow for reliable judgements to be made about the efficiency of different approaches to systematic phonics instruction (Stuart, 2006). In countries where there are one-to-one mappings between letters and sounds (e.g. Finland, Greece, Italy and Spain), there is evidence to suggest that synthetic phonics can be extremely effective (Landerl, 2000). However, the phonological complexity of the English language and the inconsistent spelling system mean that there is a need for direct instruction at levels other than that of the phoneme in order to produce effective readers (Goswami, 2005; Wyse and Goswami, 2008). The inconsist-ency of English inhibits the automatic correspondences between graphemes and their phonemes (Seymour et al., 2003), and thus it seems logical to suggest that beginning readers should be taught a range of grain sizes rather than focusing solely on the level of the phoneme. There is now a considerable body of evidence to suggest that no one method of teaching children to read is superior to any other method (Landerl, 2000; Spencer and Hanley, 2003; Torgerson et al., 2006; Walton et al., 2001), and there is no empirical evidence to justify Rose's recommendation that the teaching of reading in England should rely on synthetic phonics. Much of his evidence was anecdo-tal (Wyse and Goswami, 2008) rather than empirical, and formulating policy on the basis of anec-dotal evidence lacks sufficient rigour to justify its implementation.

However, although the evidence on the most effective approach to teaching phonics is inconclusive, there is clear evidence that a systematic approach to phonics produces gains in word reading and spelling (Torgerson et al., 2006), irrespective of whether analytic or synthetic phonics are used. Walton et al. (2001) concluded from their research that as long as tuition was systematic, then both approaches (synthetic and analytic) lead to similar gains, and this finding is supported by a range of studies (Landerl, 2000; Spencer and Hanley, 2003; Torgerson et al., 2006; Walton et al., 2001).

NEXT STEPS

The evidence suggests that no one type of phonics is necessarily more effective than another. However, what is clear from the research is that a systematic approach for teaching phonics is important, and therefore fidelity to one scheme would ensure this. Given these findings, it could be argued that one size does not fit all. Some children might master the skill of word recognition through synthetic phonics, but other approaches for teaching phonics should not be discounted, particularly if synthetic phonics has been implemented and has been unsuccessful. This has implications for weak readers in Key Stages 2 and 3 who therefore might not benefit from exposure to more synthetic phonics. It is clear that phonics is one tool within a rich toolkit. To become a skilled reader, children need access to a broad and rich language curriculum that exposes them to an exciting range of real books. Limiting children's exposure to text through providing access to decodable books will not foster a love of reading. A multisensory approach to the teaching of phonics can support the development of phoneme recognition and word reading skills.

CASE STUDY

Sally was a reception teacher. She had identified a group of children in her class who were finding it difficult to develop the skills of phoneme recognition, blending and segmenting. They struggled with grapheme–phoneme correspondence, which impacted detrimentally on their skills in phoneme recognition. To support the development of phoneme recognition skills, Sally adopted a variety of multisensory approaches in her teaching. These including tracing letters in sand and glitter, 'feeling' letter shapes made out of sandpaper, and making graphemes out of malleable materials. To support the processes of blending and segmenting (blending phonemes for reading and segmenting words into constituent phonemes for spelling), Sally used the alphabet arc. The alphabet was laid out in an arc at the top of a magnetic board. The target phoneme was positioned in the middle of the board. Children were then given a word to represent on the board by selecting the remaining letters and combining these with the target phoneme. For example, the phoneme /ai/ was positioned in the middle of the board. Children were then asked to use the remaining graphemes in the arc to represent words such as *rain, aim, jail* and *sail*. Where possible, Sally tried to alter the position of the target phoneme in the word. The magnetic letters were used to develop the skills of blending and segmenting.

Laying the foundations for phonics

It has been argued that some children might struggle with phoneme identification and the skills of blending and segmenting because they have underdeveloped auditory and visual skills, and their visual memory might also be weak (Glazzard, 2017). In addition, their phonological awareness may be underdeveloped (Glazzard, 2017). The sections below outline the implications of this for teachers.

The development of auditory skills

Auditory skills are essential for reading development. Children require the skill of auditory discrimination to differentiate between the sounds of the phonemes. If this skill is not fully developed, children will find the skill of blending difficult (Glazzard, 2017). However, before children can distinguish between phonemes, they need to be able to distinguish between environmental, musical and bodily sounds. If they can distinguish between everyday sounds, they are well placed to distinguish between phonemes when they start learning phonics. Children in the early years and Key Stage 1 who are struggling with phoneme discrimination might not require additional phonics intervention. Instead, they may require intervention in general sound discrimination.

The development of visual skills

Phonics programmes focus on the development of auditory skills. However, children also require visual skills to become good readers (Glazzard, 2017). This is because they need to distinguish between visual symbols (letters) and words. They also require visual memory skills because they need to hold and retrieve a large amount of visual information from their memory (Glazzard, 2017). The problem with only emphasising the importance of phonics in the process of reading development is that this neglects the critical role that visual awareness, visual discrimination, visual memory and visual sequential memory play in reading development. These elements are explored in the following case study.

CASE STUDY

Ameena identified a group of children who had weak visual processing skills. This was impacting detrimentally on their reading development. She planned a visual intervention programme to address this rather than providing them with additional phonics instruction. Activities included the following:

- *Visual awareness*: Sorting shapes by various criteria (e.g. colours, shape names, sizes).
- *Visual discrimination*: Odd one out activities that required children to identify the odd one out from a range of items, progressing from using objects, photographs and silhouettes.
- *Visual memory*: Presenting children with a collection of different items, asking them to close their eyes, and then removing an item. The children identify the item that has been removed, and then the complexity is increased by removing several items from a set and by including more items.
- *Visual sequential memory*: Showing the children a set of different items and then removing them from their view. The children replicate the order of the items with which they were originally presented.

How do these activities support early reading development?

The development of phonological awareness

Some children struggle to learn phonics because they have underdeveloped phonological awareness (Glazzard, 2017). Phonological awareness includes awareness of whole words, syllables, onsets and rimes, and rhyme. It is not the same thing as phonemic awareness, which is the ability to identify the separate phonemes in words. Phonological awareness develops before phonemic awareness, yet phonics programmes pay insufficient attention to its development. Children who struggle with phonemic awareness might need further intervention to develop their phonological awareness because phonological awareness is crucial for reading development. A progression sequence in children's phonological awareness is outlined below:

- Compound word blending and segmenting (e.g. car + park = car park; hairbrush = hair + brush).

- Syllable blending and segmenting (e.g. win + dow = window; jumper = jump + er).

- Onset and rime blending and segmenting (e.g. s + oap = soap) – the onset is the part of the word before the vowel, and the rime is the vowel and the rest of the word.

- Developing an awareness of rhyme (e.g. rhyme awareness, rhyme identification and rhyme generation).

- Phonemic awareness (e.g. s-p-l-a-sh).

Some children will not need to work through this development sequence because their skills in phonemic awareness will be secure. However, if children are struggling to hear phonemes within words, then this progression sequence will support their development towards phonemic awareness. Within this sequence, phonemic awareness is viewed as a skill that appears as the most complex skill because it requires children to process a greater number of sounds than blending or segmenting at the level of the whole word, syllable, or onset and rime.

What have you learned?

This chapter has introduced key research in relation to synthetic phonics. In doing so, it has emphasised the importance of schools providing children with a programme of systematic synthetic phonics instruction. The chapter has outlined key myths in relation to the teaching of phonics and highlighted the need for teachers to challenge these through their professional practice. Practical guidance has been offered to support your teaching of phonics, and the chapter has provided some consideration of phonics teaching in relation to the national and international context. Additionally, the chapter has discussed the development of phonological and phonemic awareness, and the implications of these have been outlined in relation to the delivery of phonics programmes. Some case study material has also been provided to illuminate effective practice and encourage you to reflect on your existing provision.

——— FURTHER READING ———

Joliffe, W., Waugh, D. and Gill, A. (2019) *Teaching Systematic Synthetic Phonics in Primary Schools.* London: SAGE.

Waugh, D., Carter, J. and Desmond, C. (2015) *Lessons in Teaching Phonics in Primary Schools.* London: SAGE.

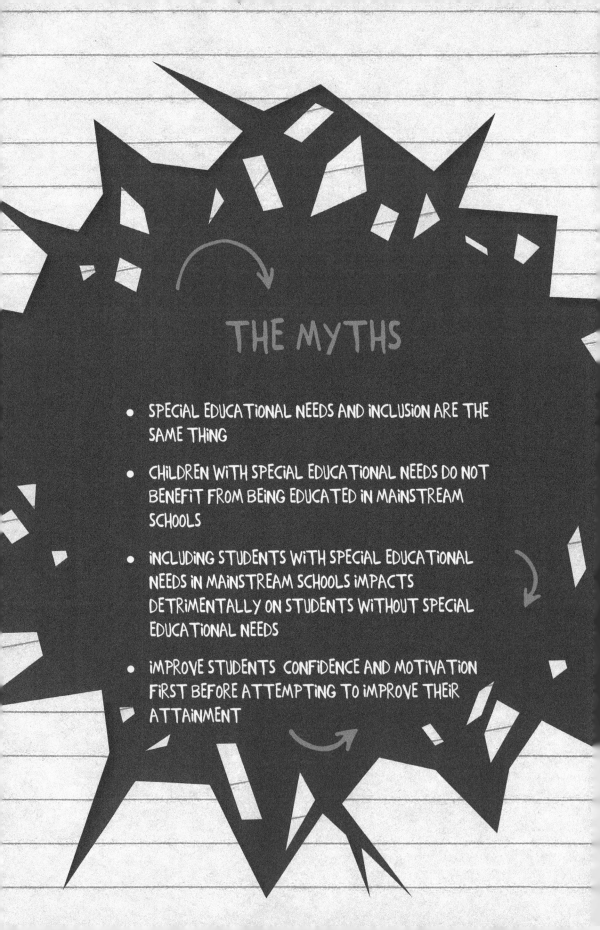

THE MYTHS

- SPECIAL EDUCATIONAL NEEDS AND INCLUSION ARE THE SAME THING

- CHILDREN WITH SPECIAL EDUCATIONAL NEEDS DO NOT BENEFIT FROM BEING EDUCATED IN MAINSTREAM SCHOOLS

- INCLUDING STUDENTS WITH SPECIAL EDUCATIONAL NEEDS IN MAINSTREAM SCHOOLS IMPACTS DETRIMENTALLY ON STUDENTS WITHOUT SPECIAL EDUCATIONAL NEEDS

- IMPROVE STUDENTS CONFIDENCE AND MOTIVATION FIRST BEFORE ATTEMPTING TO IMPROVE THEIR ATTAINMENT

14

iNCLUSiON AND SPECiAL EDUCATiONAL NEEDS

What will you learn?

This chapter outlines myths relating to inclusion and special educational needs. Specifically, it explores the difference between these terms while also considering the wider context in relation to mainstream schooling and students without special educational needs. Some practical guidance is also offered to support you to reflect on your existing provision. Additionally, the chapter outlines relevant research and emphasises the importance of teachers challenging myths within their professional practice. Some practical case study material is provided to illustrate effective practice in relation to inclusion and special educational needs.

——— WHAT ARE THE MYTHS? ———

- Special educational needs and inclusion are the same thing.
- Children with special educational needs do not benefit from being educated in mainstream schools.
- Including students with special educational needs in mainstream schools impacts detrimentally on students without special educational needs.
- Improve students' confidence and motivation first before attempting to improve their attainment.

Why should teachers challenge the myths?

Teachers are required by law to have regard to the principles of the code of practice for special educational needs and disabilities (DfE and DoH, 2015). It is often assumed that the implementation of the code will facilitate inclusion, and the term 'special educational needs' is often associated with inclusion. This chapter demonstrates that this is a myth. There is also a common assumption that students with special educational needs require a different approach to teaching (i.e. pedagogy), and teachers often rely on the guidance offered by external specialist professionals to support them in planning to meet the needs of specific students. This chapter challenges this assumption. Often it is thought that students with special educational needs and disabilities are better suited to special schools rather than mainstream schools, and it is sometimes assumed that issues of low confidence and low motivation should be addressed before teaching them subject content. The problem with all of these assumptions is that they result in low outcomes for specific groups of learners. Too many students with special educational needs do not go on to gain qualifications or access further education, employment or independent living. Outcomes for different groups of students are also variable.

KEY RESEARCH

SPECIAL EDUCATIONAL NEEDS AND INCLUSION ARE THE SAME THING

It has been argued that inclusive education must be disassociated from special educational needs so that it is able, as a separate policy discourse, to articulate its distinct values of social justice, democracy and equity (Slee, 2011). Inclusive education necessitates a departure from traditional processes that label, segregate and stigmatise children to enable schools to embrace diversity (Graham and Harwood, 2011). The processes of early identification, labelling, individualised learning, intervention and monitoring are deeply embedded throughout the code of practice (Glazzard, 2013). They reflect a pathological model through which 'abnormalities' are identified, diagnosed, treated and cured. These processes categorise children by their differences and are rooted in a psycho-medical paradigm that 'conceptualizes difficulties in learning as arising from deficits in the neurological or psychological make-up of the child' (Skidmore, 2004, p2). According to Allan (2008), 'these mechanisms of surveillance create subjects who are known and marked in particular kinds of ways' (p87).

Labels ascribe to individuals a minority status that presumes a weakness and vulnerability compared with their peers (Thomas and Loxley, 2007). Essentially, they create an othering effect through separating out learners. In addition, the concept of 'need' reinforces notions of deficit and disadvantage (Thomas and Loxley, 2007), and locates the cause of the deficiency within the child rather than in systemic factors that produce exclusion. The use of the word 'special' within the lexicon of special needs is also problematic because it names difference and makes it visible. Labels are socially produced and socially assigned, and children who deviate from social norms are assigned identities that stigmatise, marginalise and separate them from their peers. The code uses words such as 'challenging', 'disruptive' or 'disturbing' to describe students' behaviour, all of which are deeply offensive and serve to reinforce feelings of abnormality.

It has been argued that the code promotes a 'highly individualised approach' (Skidmore, 2004, p15) which locates the deficiencies within the child rather than the deficiencies within the school or broader education system (Dyson, 2001). The use of intervention groups, classroom withdrawal, and involvement of specialist professionals serve to perpetuate segregation and result in children becoming objects of scrutiny. Additionally, teaching assistants form part of a package of support for students identified as having special educational needs. The 'reward', it would seem, for being labelled is to be denied access to a qualified teacher for all of the time. These processes mark these children out by their differences, restrict equality of opportunity, and assign on to individuals an inferior status rather than promoting inclusion (Dunne, 2009).

Inclusion originally evolved as a policy agenda to transform the education system. The current education system privileges specific types of academic knowledge. Schools are evaluated on a restricted range of academic performance indicators. Students whose achievement and behaviour fall outside of a permitted normative boundary are often labelled as having special educational needs. For inclusion to be achieved, it is necessary to transform the structures that underpin the education system. The processes of diagnosis, categorisation and intervention that are so deeply embedded within the code of practice do not align with the values of inclusion because they create othering. The curriculum needs to be transformed to meet the needs of all learners. A reconceptualisation of what is meant by 'achievement' is also necessary to promote inclusion. This necessitates a radical overhaul of the assessment system, which currently privileges academic attainment.

It can therefore be argued that inclusion and special educational needs are not comfortable bedfellows. The processes within the code of practice need to be interrogated critically.

Children with special educational needs do not benefit from being educated in mainstream schools

Research demonstrates there is strong evidence that students with disabilities benefit academically from inclusive education in mainstream schools (Hehir et al., 2016). Multiple systematic reviews indicate that students with disabilities who were educated in mainstream classes academically outperformed their peers who had been educated in segregated settings (Price, 2018). Research demonstrates that participating in inclusive mainstream education can result in social and emotional benefits for students with disabilities (Hehir et al., 2016). According to research, 'segregated classrooms or schools perpetuate the misconception that individuals with disabilities are fundamentally different from their nondisabled peers and need to be isolated or separated' (Hayes and Bulat, 2017, p6).

Dyssegaard and Larsen (2013) found that students who attended mainstream schools had better academic achievements, improved wellbeing and better peer relationships than those who attended special schools. It was also found that special school settings can be more suitable for older students with special educational needs because in these settings they do not feel less competent than their peers. Therefore, the suitability of different school settings (mainstream or special) is affected by the age of students as well as the specific nature of their needs (Dyssegaard and Larsen, 2013).

Including students with special educational needs in mainstream schools impacts detrimentally on students without special educational needs

Research demonstrates that students without special educational needs are not negatively affected when students with special educational needs are included in the mainstream classroom (Dyssegaard and Larsen, 2013). Thus, being educated alongside a student with a disability does not lead to adverse effects for non-disabled children (Price, 2018). Research also demonstrates that where students with special educational needs are included in mainstream classrooms, non-disabled peers often hold less prejudicial views and are more accepting of people who are different from themselves (Price, 2018). It has been argued that:

> Decades of research in the United States and other high-income countries have demonstrated that inclusive education benefits not only students with disabilities but also students without disabilities. Inclusive classrooms teach all students about the importance of diversity and acceptance. Evidence also indicates that students with and without disabilities who are educated in inclusive classrooms have better academic outcomes than students who are educated in non-inclusive classrooms.

> (Hayes and Bulat, 2017, p5)

Hehir et al. (2016) found that the overall quality of teaching in a school plays a more significant role in shaping the achievement of non-disabled students than whether or not that student was educated alongside children with special educational needs.

Improve students' confidence and motivation first before attempting to improve their attainment

It has been argued that:

> Teachers who are confronted with the poor motivation and confidence of low attaining students may interpret this as the cause of their low attainment and assume that it is both necessary and possible to address their motivation before attempting to teach them new material. In fact, the evidence shows that attempts to enhance motivation in this way are unlikely to achieve that end. Even if they do, the impact on subsequent learning is close to zero .... In fact, the poor motivation of low attainers is a logical response to repeated failure. Start getting them to succeed and their motivation and confidence should increase.

> (Coe et al., 2014, p23)

CASE STUDY

The senior leadership team of a secondary school recently reviewed its policies and procedures in relation to assessing and identifying young people with special educational needs and disabilities. As part of this review, the senior leadership team took steps to further develop existing relationships with feeder schools. This formalisation of the transition process supported the school to access information that was held by previous providers and to collect this information prior to children joining the school.

At Key Stage 3, the process of identification now starts much earlier than it had previously. The new process involves the school liaising with feeder schools and distributing a pro forma to capture key information. The school uses this information to determine the nature and structure of the annual transition process. When children are identified as having special educational needs and disabilities, they are offered an opportunity to visit the school prior to officially starting. In some cases, this visit has taken place with parents or carers. In other cases, it has involved children spending one week in the school setting prior to their official start. Some children have also been assigned a transition mentor to support their transition from one setting to another.

NEXT STEPS

The code of practice for special educational needs and disabilities (DfE and DoH, 2015) emphasises the importance of working in partnership with children, young people, and parents and carers. It is important to involve these stakeholders in key decision-making processes, including setting targets to support the child's development and reviewing progress. Too often young people are not consulted about their needs and key decisions are made without consultation with students.

It is important to have high expectations of all children, including those with special educational needs and disabilities. This is emphasised within the code of practice. You should ensure that you provide all learners with an appropriate level of challenge. Too often expectations and challenge are too low for students with special educational needs, and consequently they do not always achieve their full educational potential. Like all students, learners with special educational needs benefit from frequent opportunities to revisit prior learning, and retrieval exercises are a useful strategy to ensure that knowledge, skills and attitudes are embedded within the long-term memory. Reviewing previous learning leads to much greater long-term retention if subject content is spread out, with gaps in between to allow students to forget the content. This 'is one of the most general and robust effects from across the entire history of experimental research on learning and memory' (Bjork and Bjork, 2011, p59). Many students benefit from repeated exposure to subject content, particularly when content is spaced out and revisited rather than taught in a single block and never revisited. All students benefit from a curriculum that develops social and emotional literacy and regulation skills (Roffey, 2017), and this is particularly important for learners with special educational needs. These points demonstrate that high-quality inclusive teaching which also embeds these elements, along with frequent assessment and feedback, benefits all learners. Students with special educational needs do not always need a differentiated pedagogy; they need access to the same high-quality teaching that benefits everyone.

It is also important to broaden your understanding of inclusion beyond disability. You will need to consider the inclusion of individuals who belong to vulnerable groups, including those with non-normative gender identities and sexualities, students living in poverty, second language learners, and

(Continued)

(Continued)

students who belong to a minority ethnic or racial group. You will need to maintain high expectations of all learners. The school and classroom environment should reflect students' broad range of identities. The resources that you use within your teaching (e.g. the texts that you read) should reflect the students' identities, particularly in relation to their social and cultural backgrounds. You will also need to be aware that identities are intersectional, and therefore students do not always fit neatly into one category. It is important to be aware that some students may be experiencing multiple forms of disadvantage which can impact not only on their wellbeing, but also on their behaviour and academic attainment.

Crucially, it is important to look beyond assigned labels. Students are, first and foremost, individuals. The problem with labels is that there is a tendency for teachers to apply 'off-the-shelf' strategies to students with particular needs. A child who has a diagnosis of autism may not require access to a visual timetable, despite the fact that this is a common suggested strategy for learners within this group. A child with dyslexia does not necessarily require their worksheets to be printed on blue paper, and they may not benefit from the use of coloured overlays when reading text. A child with challenging behaviour may not benefit from an individual reward system. Although these strategies may work for some students, they will not work for all, and learners who share the same label may have very different needs. Your role as a teacher is to respond to the needs of the child rather than responding to a label. Consult the child and their parents or carers to find out what strategies might help. You do not need to be an expert in the needs of all of the different groups of children. Find out as much as you can about the strengths and needs of each student and be prepared to take advice from colleagues. Above all, be confident that you can educate all children regardless of their diverse characteristics.

CASE STUDY

The governing body of a primary school has taken steps to increase the involvement of parents and carers, and to offer opportunities for this involvement as early as possible. Staff now have formal and informal mechanisms in place to gather information from parents and carers in relation to their needs and any support that has been found to be valuable at home or within previous settings. A home liaison worker has also been employed to support this communication and to establish a 'voice forum' for the parents and carers of children with special educational needs and disabilities.

What have you learned?

This chapter has outlined myths relating to inclusion and special educational needs. Specifically, it has explored the difference between these terms while also considering the wider context in relation to mainstream schooling and students without special educational needs. Some practical guidance has been offered to support you to reflect on your existing provision. Additionally, the chapter has outlined relevant research and emphasised the importance of teachers challenging myths within their professional practice. Some practical case study material has been provided to illustrate effective practice in relation to inclusion and special educational needs.

FURTHER READING

Delaney, M. (2016) *Special Educational Needs*. Oxford: Oxford University Press.

Packer, N. (2016) *The Teachers Guide to SEN*. Carmarthen: Crown House Publishing.

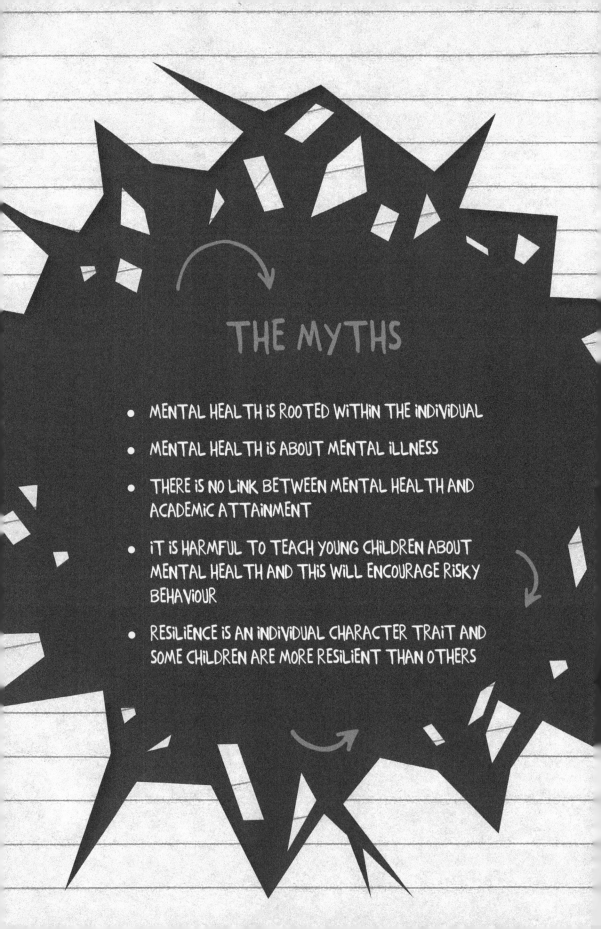

THE MYTHS

- MENTAL HEALTH IS ROOTED WITHIN THE INDIVIDUAL

- MENTAL HEALTH IS ABOUT MENTAL ILLNESS

- THERE IS NO LINK BETWEEN MENTAL HEALTH AND ACADEMIC ATTAINMENT

- IT IS HARMFUL TO TEACH YOUNG CHILDREN ABOUT MENTAL HEALTH AND THIS WILL ENCOURAGE RISKY BEHAVIOUR

- RESILIENCE IS AN INDIVIDUAL CHARACTER TRAIT AND SOME CHILDREN ARE MORE RESILIENT THAN OTHERS

15
MENTAL HEALTH

What will you learn?

This chapter outlines a range of myths in relation to mental health, and discusses these within the context of society, mental illness, academic attainment, harm and resilience. The chapter emphasises the importance of teachers challenging these myths through their professional practice, and we also argue that schools play a crucial role in supporting children's mental health. However, the chapter also explains that teachers are not therapists or counsellors, and cannot and should not seek to provide the same level of care or intervention as a trained clinician. Some practical guidance is offered to support you to reflect on your professional practice, and we outline the importance of schools adopting a whole-school approach to mental health.

WHAT ARE THE MYTHS?

- Mental health is rooted within the individual.
- Mental health is about mental illness.
- There is no link between mental health and academic attainment.
- It is harmful to teach young children about mental health and this will encourage risky behaviour.
- Resilience is an individual character trait and some children are more resilient than others.

Why should teachers challenge the myths?

Studies report increasing numbers of children and young people experiencing self-harm, anxiety, phobias, depression, substance misuse, post-traumatic stress syndrome, and attachment, hyperkinetic, conduct, developmental and eating disorders (DfE, 2014; Dickins, 2014; Sisak et al., 2014; Wolke et al., 2013). Long waiting lists for children and young people to access specialist health services and stringent referral criteria mean that many do not receive timely support, and many are denied access to these services. Within this context, schools play an important role in supporting children's mental health. However, it is important to emphasise that teachers are not therapists or counsellors. They are specialists in education. They do not have clinical training. There are limits to what schools can be expected to do, but nonetheless they play a role in delivering educational interventions that improve students' wellbeing and mental health literacy.

KEY RESEARCH

MENTAL HEALTH iS RooTED WiTHiN THE iNDiViDUAL

Social changes within the twenty-first century include income inequality, parental conflict and relationship breakdown, parental health, school, and technology-related factors. Evidence suggests that these can all have a negative impact on young people's mental health (Bor et al., 2014; The Children's Society, 2014).

The research cited above demonstrates that mental ill health is rooted in social circumstances rather than within individuals. Although experiences of disability can increase the likelihood of developing mental ill health (Glazzard, 2019), adverse social circumstances, including poverty, contribute to or cause poor mental health. This demonstrates that causation does not reside within the individual, but within a broader ecological framework which includes the school, family, community and policy context, all of which shape the lives of individuals. Intervention at the level of the individual child or young person will therefore not solve the mental health 'crisis'. A political response is needed to tackle the systemic causes of poor mental health.

Mental health is about mental illness

Mental health sits along a continuum, with mental health at one end and severe mental illness at the other. According to Prever (2006), it is important that young people understand everyone's mental health sits somewhere on that continuum, and there will be times in our lives when we might require additional help. Mental health work in schools should therefore not solely focus on mental illness. Children and young people need to be taught about how to remain mentally healthy. They need to be able to recognise how their own mental health might change and they need to be taught strategies to remain mentally healthy.

There is no link between mental health and academic attainment

The links between mental health, academic success and life opportunities have been established in published research studies (Clausson and Berg, 2008; Cushman et al., 2011; Ekornes et al., 2012). Thus, schools have a vested interest in supporting young people's mental health. A large body of research suggests that school-based interventions which support students' social-emotional development can positively affect academic outcomes (Greenberg et al., 2003; Gumora and Arsenio, 2002; Malecki and Elliott, 2002; Zins et al., 2004). This suggests that there is an association between social and emotional development (or wellbeing) and mental health.

It is harmful to teach young children about mental health and will encourage risky behaviour

Recent evidence suggests that teaching young people about mental health improves their mental health literacy, including their knowledge of how to stay mentally healthy and how to get support, rather than causing any harmful effects (Glazzard, 2019). Research suggests that the attitudes of young people can be changed more easily than those of adults (Corrigan and Watson, 2007), and therefore schools can play a critical role in eradicating stigma in relation to mental health (Glazzard, 2019).

Research by Danby and Hamilton (2016) suggests that primary school practitioners are reluctant to use the term 'mental health' with young children. Some practitioners associated the term 'mental health' with stigma, some linked mental health directly with mental illness, and others felt that softer terminology, including 'feelings' and 'emotions', was more appropriate (Danby and Hamilton, 2016). The desire to protect young children from the language of mental health is a concern because it suggests that mental health is a negative attribute within an individual. This does nothing to eradicate the stigma that has been associated with mental health, but simply perpetuates it. If practitioners can talk to young people about their physical health, then there is no reason why mental health should not become part of the child's lexicon.

Resilience is an individual character trait and some children are more resilient than others

Research suggests that although some protective factors for resilience are rooted within the individual (Werner, 2000), many are located within the social contexts in which children live and learn (Roffey, 2017). Resilience is a multidimensional construct, and therefore it is possible to be more or less resilient when operating within different contexts. Resilience is also relational (Roffey, 2017). Children who have access to strong social support networks (friends and family) and are exposed to a positive school culture that provides a sense of belonging often have greater resilience than those who do not. Although resilience is often understood as the ability of the individual to 'bounce back' from situations of adversity, this over-simplistic understanding of resilience neglects the fact that for some, situations of adversity are permanent rather than temporary (Roffey, 2017). The focus on school-based interventions that aim to improve young people's resilience therefore neglects the impact of the social, cultural and political contexts which influence their lives. Resilience should therefore be understood within the context of an ecological model rather than being attributed solely to the individual.

CASE STUDY

A primary school ran an annual 'wellbeing day' to raise the profile of mental health. The children listened to presentations about how to look after their own mental health and a range of activities were planned to promote positive wellbeing. These included workshops on mindfulness, dance and a variety of other forms of physical activity, music, art, and cookery classes that promoted healthy eating. The children were taught about the importance of water for hydration and the benefits of physical activity. Activities were also planned to support the wellbeing of staff and parents and carers.

NEXT STEPS

Schools play an important role in supporting children and young people to be mentally healthy. The model of the whole school approach to mental health by Public Health England is outlined in Figure 1.

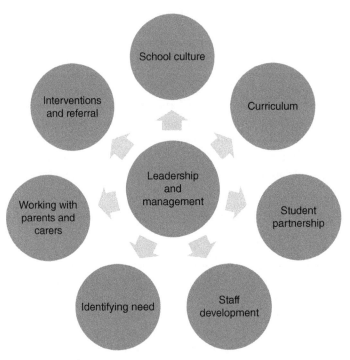

Figure 1 Whole-school approach to mental health (PHE, 2015)

Central to the whole-school approach to mental health is the prioritisation of mental health by the school leadership team. For the whole-school approach to be effective, leaders need to view mental health as a strategic priority. It therefore needs to be a standing item for discussion at leadership and governor meetings and it needs to be supported by a written policy.

A positive school culture promotes a sense of belonging that enables young people to be mentally healthy. As a teacher, you will need to reflect on the quality of relationships in your classroom. If relationships between you and the students and between the students themselves are positive, this will support young people to be mentally healthy. Central to this is the valuing of diversity within the school and classroom so that everyone experiences a sense of belonging regardless of individual differences.

Children need a mental health curriculum to support them in staying mentally healthy. With younger students, this is likely to focus on developing children's emotional and social literacy and regulation. Roffey's (2017) work has emphasised the importance of social and emotional learning for children. Young children need to be taught to recognise and manage their feelings and to understand the social skills that are required in different contexts. As pupils progress through schools, they need a well-sequenced curriculum that develops their mental health literacy and supports them in developing resilience and character. Activities that promote mindfulness (enjoying being within the present) may also help to reduce anxiety and create a calm atmosphere in the classroom.

The role of students as partners is emphasised within the framework of the whole-school approach (PHE, 2015). As 'mental health' is now part of a category of need in the code of practice for special educational needs and/or disabilities (DfE and DoH, 2015), you will need to ensure that you consult children with mental health needs by involving them in setting targets for their development and in reviewing their progress. In addition, you will need to involve parents and carers in the same processes, considering that they may also have mental health or other special educational needs or disabilities. Schools might wish to consider providing mental health workshops for parents and carers and signposting them to appropriate sources of support.

The identification of mental health needs is important because the sooner children get the right support, the less chance there is of a problem spiralling out of control. You should look out for common signs, including sudden changes in a child's mood or their behaviour, a declining academic profile, or evidence that the child is becoming withdrawn. All staff working within a school need to be trained to identify the signs and symptoms of mental ill health. However, you should also remember that many needs may remain hidden, so it is important to provide children with frequent opportunities to talk about their feelings. Some primary schools use a 'feelings' board that provides an opportunity for children to put their names next to a symbol (usually a face) which best represents how they feel. You can then follow this up with individuals who have negative feelings. Some schools have confidential 'worry boxes' that allow primary school children to post a message to their teachers. Secondary schools are more likely to use commercial self-assessment questionnaires that specifically explore different aspects of wellbeing with students. These are signposted in the 'further reading' section at the end of the chapter.

Schools should plan a range of interventions to support students' mental health needs. These should include universal interventions that are available to all students, group interventions for students with common needs, and targeted interventions for students with highly specific needs. The impact of interventions should be measured using an appropriate assessment tool that best fits the intervention, and the use of pre- and post-assessments is recommended.

CASE STUDY

A secondary school planned an intervention to develop students' mental health literacy. The Year 8 students were provided with an eight-week intervention that addressed different aspects of mental health. Sessions included background information explaining mental health, information on managing stress, anxiety and depression, and mindfulness. One of the sessions focused on the effects of social media on mental health, and students were introduced to the concept of digital citizenship. All students undertaking the programme also completed a training course

(Continued)

(Continued)

on how to be a good listener, which qualified them to apply for the role of student mental health champion. The champions were then assigned to younger students who needed someone to talk to. The school used a mental health literacy survey that they had developed to measure students' knowledge of mental health before and after the intervention. The results from this demonstrated significant improvements in students' mental health literacy. They had developed a greater under-standing of mental health, learned strategies for managing their own mental health, and knew how to get help if they needed it.

What have you learned?

This chapter has outlined a range of myths in relation to mental health, and discussed these within the context of society, mental illness, academic attainment, harm and resilience. The chapter has also emphasised the importance of teachers challenging these myths through their professional practice, and we have argued that schools play a crucial role in supporting children's mental health. However, the chapter has also explained that teachers are not therapists or counsellors, and cannot and should not seek to provide the same level of care or intervention as a trained clinician. Some practical guidance has been offered to support you to reflect on your professional practice, and we have outlined the importance of schools adopting a whole-school approach to mental health.

—— FURTHER READING ——

Evidence Based Practice Unit (EBPU) (n.d.) *Learning from HeadStart: Wellbeing Measurement Framework for Primary Schools.* Available at: www.corc.uk.net/media/1506/primary-school-measures_310317_forweb.pdf

Evidence Based Practice Unit (EBPU) (n.d.) *Learning from HeadStart: Wellbeing Measurement Framework for Secondary Schools.* Available at: www.corc.uk.net/media/1517/blf17_20-second-school-measuresbl-17-03-17b.pdf

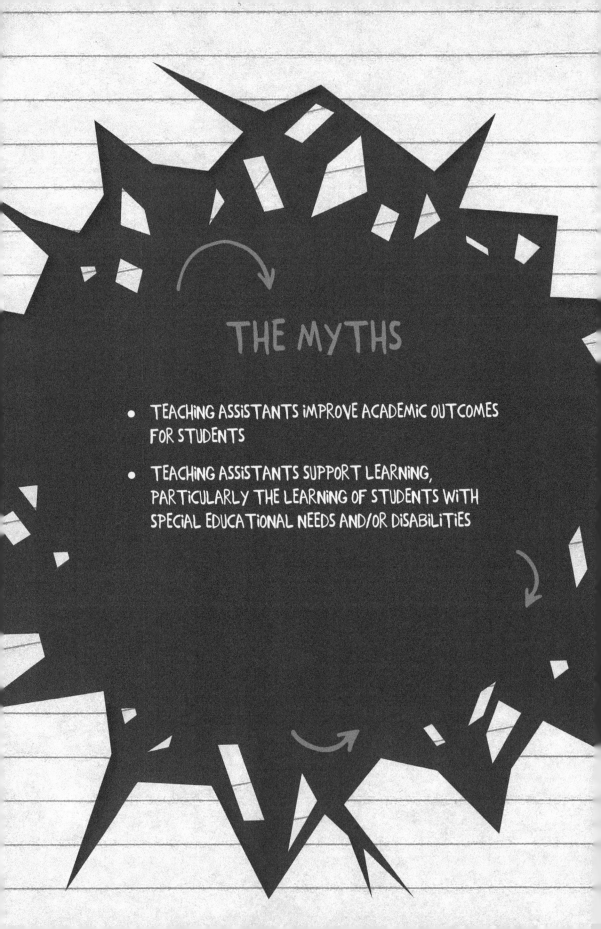

THE MYTHS

- TEACHING ASSISTANTS IMPROVE ACADEMIC OUTCOMES FOR STUDENTS

- TEACHING ASSISTANTS SUPPORT LEARNING, PARTICULARLY THE LEARNING OF STUDENTS WITH SPECIAL EDUCATIONAL NEEDS AND/OR DISABILITIES

16
TEACHING ASSISTANTS

What will you learn?

Teaching assistants (TAs) make up approximately 34 per cent of the primary workforce and 15 per cent of the secondary workforce (Sharples et al., 2015). There has been a sharp rise in the number of teaching assistants over the past 15 years, and therefore the expenditure associated with this is significant. This chapter presents the latest research into the deployment of teaching assistants and their impact (Sharples et al., 2015). We will challenge some myths associated with teaching assistant deployment and identify some key implications for practice.

WHAT ARE THE MYTHS?

- Teaching assistants improve academic outcomes for students.
- Teaching assistants support learning, particularly the learning of students with special educational needs and/or disabilities.

Why should teachers challenge the myths?

It is important that teachers do not take these assumptions for granted because it is the teacher who is accountable for students' academic outcomes and their learning, not the teaching assistant. Teachers therefore need to ensure that deployment arrangements for teaching assistants are enabling students to learn more effectively, resulting in improved outcomes for students.

KEY RESEARCH

Research demonstrates that teaching assistants spend the majority of their time supporting students with the highest level of need (Sharples et al., 2015). This limits opportunities for peer interaction and limits exposure to high-quality teaching by the teacher. Research demonstrates that the quality of instruction which students receive from teaching assistants is inferior to that provided by the teacher (Radford et al., 2011; Rubie-Davies et al., 2010). For example, evidence suggests that teaching assistants tend to close down talk and 'spoon-feed' answers (Radford et al., 2011; Rubie-Davies et al., 2010). Over time, this can limit understanding, weaken pupils' sense of control over their learning, and reduce their capacity to develop independent learning skills (Sharples et al., 2015). According to Sharples et al. (2015):

> Those pupils receiving the most support from TAs made less progress than similar pupils who received little or no support from TAs. There was also evidence that the negative impact was most marked for pupils with the highest levels of SEN, who, as discussed, typically receive the most TA support.

(p12)

Evidence suggests that some deployment arrangements can foster student dependency rather than promoting independent learning, largely because they prioritise task completion rather than encouraging pupils to think for themselves (Moyles and Suschitzky, 1997). In addition, the over-reliance on one-to-one teaching assistant support can lead to lack of ownership and responsibility for learning, as well as separation from peers (Giangreco, 2010). Research demonstrates that the average impact of teaching assistants delivering structured interventions is less than that for interventions using experienced qualified teachers (Sharples et al., 2015).

Research also suggests that although teaching assistants can have positive effects in relation to reducing teacher workload and reducing classroom disruption, levels of qualifications vary between teaching assistants, and opportunities for communication between teaching assistants and teachers can be minimal (Blatchford et al., 2012). This means that teaching assistants can be underprepared when they go into classrooms.

CASE STUDY

A school-based mentor in a secondary school delivered an inset session on the deployment of teaching assistants. This session was delivered to all new teaching staff as part of the school's induction programme. Teaching staff were asked to reflect on how they deploy teaching assistants at all stages of a lesson. During the session, there was a specific focus on the deployment arrangements at the start and end of lessons. This focus was prioritised as the mentor felt that deployment during these times was often less effective as teaching assistants are often simply listening to the teacher talk.

The teaching staff worked together to identify strategies for the effective deployment of teaching assistants during the introduction and closing stages of a lesson. In summary, the strategies that were discussed included:

- breaking down an aspect of subject content for a pupil using a small whiteboard;
- monitoring a child's behaviour and engagement to ensure that they focus on you;
- assessing pupils' responses to the teaching, noting down which pupils develop misconceptions;
- working individually with pupils who were absent in the previous lesson to ensure that they catch up;
- supporting a group of pupils who do not need to listen to the main teaching input (e.g. pupils working at a higher stage of development or those working at a lower stage);
- team-teaching the lesson with you.

NEXT STEPS

The following recommendations will support the effective deployment of teaching assistants:

- Teaching assistants should not be used as an informal teaching resource for low-attaining pupils.
- Deploy teaching assistants to add value to what teachers do, not replace them.
- Deploy teaching assistants to support the development of students' independent learning skills and help students to manage their own learning.
- Ensure that teaching assistants are fully prepared for their role in the classroom.
- Deploy teaching assistants to deliver high-quality one-to-one and small group support using structured interventions.
- Adopt evidence-based interventions to support teaching assistants in their small group and one-to-one instruction.
- Ensure explicit connections are made between learning from everyday classroom teaching and structured interventions.

(Sharples et al., 2015)

Teachers should ensure that they teach all students frequently. Often those students with the highest level of need spend a lot of their time working with the teaching assistant rather than with the teachers. The evidence from the research stated in this chapter suggests that this can limit opportunities for independent thinking and foster a culture of dependency. As a teacher, it is important that you teach students with the highest levels of need. The code of practice for special educational needs and/or disabilities (DfE and DoH, 2015) explicitly emphasises that the teaching assistant forms part of a package of support for students with specific needs, but they should never replace the teacher. The accountability for the student outcomes rests with you, not the teaching assistant.

Sometimes it might be appropriate for the teaching assistant to monitor the learning of the rest of the class so that you can provide targeted teaching to those learners with the highest levels

(Continued)

(Continued)

of need. Where appropriate, the tasks that you set students should not be overly differentiated, resulting in them achieving different learning outcomes. This serves to widen the ability gap and limits the achievements of learners with special educational needs. Instead, consider how you might further break down a task or provide students with additional resources and/or support to enable them to broadly achieve the same learning outcomes as their peers. The level of challenge to which you expose learners should be high, regardless of their individual needs.

An effective strategy is to lead from the front. Teach the whole class the same content but strategically position the teaching assistant with specific students so that they can further break down the content for them if necessary. This ensures that all students benefit from exposure to your teaching. Sending groups of students out of class to work with a teaching assistant on general lesson content simply limits their exposure to the teacher and creates within-class segregation. Where it is necessary to differentiate tasks so that different students are working towards different learning outcomes, it is essential that the set tasks are challenging. They must require learners to think hard, and you should expect students to demonstrate independent thinking.

Ensure that you provide clear instructions to the teaching assistant, prior to the lesson if possible. They need to understand the intended learning outcomes, what their role is during the lesson, the subject content, and the questions they need to ask during the lesson. Crucially, teaching assistants need to understand how to break down the subject content if this is required. It is important for teachers and teaching assistants to have time to communicate about these aspects of the lesson content. Some schools have adjusted the working times of teaching assistants to accommodate this. It is also important that teaching assistants have time to communicate with teachers about the progress of specific students they have been working with in the lesson. This will support the teacher in planning the next lesson, particularly if they know the misconceptions that students may have developed. In some instances, time for teaching assistants and teachers to plan collaboratively is also effective because it ensures that teaching assistants are fully prepared for their role. In addition, teaching assistants are likely to have useful knowledge about specific pupils that can be shared with teachers through collaborative planning sessions.

The evidence from research suggests that deployment arrangements are more effective when teaching assistants deliver structured interventions rather than providing students with general in-class support (Sharples et al., 2015). However, the timing of these interventions is critical because if they are implemented during lesson time, this can limit students' learning as they will miss out on subject content that is being covered by the teacher. Sometimes it will be necessary to remove students from lessons to enable them to undertake interventions. However, interventions should be time-limited so that students can rejoin the class as quickly as possible. Teachers should be clear about what students are learning during intervention sessions so that they can build on this learning within the context of classroom lessons. Too often links are not made between the learning that students undertake in interventions and classroom-based learning. Teaching assistants are likely to have greater impact on students' learning if they are trained to deliver the intervention. Given that the research indicates interventions have more impact on student outcomes when delivered by teachers, it might be possible for qualified teachers to deliver structured interventions, although this is not always a practical solution, given their responsibilities in relation to general classroom teaching. It is therefore critical that teaching assistants undertake a programme of training in the delivery of specific interventions. In addition, the quality of the delivery of interventions should be monitored through the normal school processes for monitoring teaching and learning.

Effective interventions are characterised by the following recommendations taken directly from Sharples et al. (2015):

- Sessions are often brief (20–50 minutes), occur regularly (three to five times per week) and are maintained over a sustained period (8–20 weeks). Careful timetabling is in place to enable consistent delivery.
- TAs receive extensive training from experienced trainers and/or teachers.
- The intervention has structured supporting resources and lesson plans, with clear objectives and possibly a delivery script.
- Ensure there is fidelity to the programme and do not depart from suggested delivery protocols.
- Ensure TAs closely follow the plan and structure of the intervention and use delivery scripts.
- Assessments are used to identify appropriate pupils, guide areas for focus and track pupil progress. Effective interventions ensure that the right support is being provided to the right child.
- Connections are made between the out-of-class learning in the intervention and classroom teaching.

(p24)

Evidence suggests that small group interventions can be as effective as one-to-one interventions (Sharples et al., 2015). The use of pre- and post-assessments can support teachers and school leaders to evaluate the impact of interventions on students' learning. Often interventions are commercially produced schemes that are expensive to purchase. It is important that the interventions are having the desired impact on students' learning to be able to justify the expenditure. However, the long-term impact of interventions is rarely captured by schools. If the assessments are conducted immediately after an intervention, this will not help to demonstrate if the learning gains are sustained six months after an intervention has finished. In order to ascertain learning gains, it is necessary to establish whether students are, in the long-term, able to make connections between the learning they have undertaken during the intervention and the learning that they undertake within the context of lessons. Essentially, students need to be able to apply their learning from the intervention to their classroom-based learning.

CASE STUDY

Three primary schools worked together to provide a professional development day for teachers and teaching assistants. This day provided an opportunity for staff to work together and discuss effective practice. The day was supported by a lecturer from a local university who was responsible for delivering the university's PGCert SENco qualification. The programme enabled teachers

(Continued)

(Continued)

and teaching assistants to explore their roles in relation to best practice and discuss approaches to supporting one another within a classroom setting. The lecturer provided case study material to support staff to understand examples of poor practice in relation to the deployment of teaching assistants. Teaching assistants were also given an opportunity to discuss the challenges they faced, and teachers were asked to consider solutions to address these. Teachers and teaching assistants were asked to reflect on and discuss the following questions in relation to their own practice:

- What does effective deployment look like in a classroom environment?
- How can teachers support teaching assistants to improve their impact on pupil progress?
- How can teaching assistants support teachers to improve their impact on pupil progress?
- At what points in the lesson is the deployment likely to be more effective than at other times? What is the reason for this?

What have you learned?

This chapter has introduced key research in relation to the deployment of teaching assistants. It has highlighted the key myths in relation to deployment, and we have explained that it is important teachers address these through their professional practice. The chapter has also provided some case study material to illuminate effective practice, and practical guidance has been offered to support teachers to maximise the impact of their teaching assistants in relation to pupil progress. There has been a specific focus on their deployment during the start and end of a lesson, and some questions have been provided to encourage you to reflect on your existing provision.

—— FURTHER READING

Blatchford, P., Russell, A. and Webster, R. (2012) *Reassessing the Impact of Teaching Assistants: How Research Challenges Practice and Policy.* London: Routledge.

Webster, R., Russell, A. and Blatchford, P. (2015) *Maximising the Impact of Teaching Assistants.* London: Routledge.

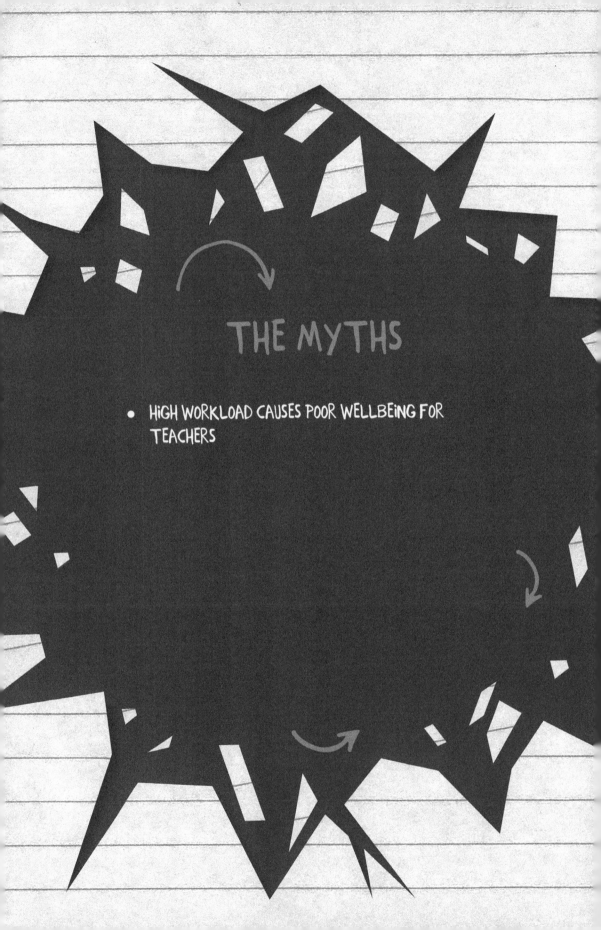

THE MYTHS

- HIGH WORKLOAD CAUSES POOR WELLBEING FOR TEACHERS

17

TEACHER WELLBEING

What will you learn?

This chapter introduces you to some of the factors that impact detrimentally on the wellbeing of teachers. These include the impact of school culture, personal circumstances and workload. Teacher resilience and teacher agency are also considered in this chapter. The chapter argues that high workload may have a detrimental effect on the wellbeing of teachers but it is not the only contributory factor.

WHAT ARE THE MYTHS?

- High workload causes poor wellbeing for teachers.

Why should teachers challenge the myths?

Educational policies (DfE, 2018; Ofsted, 2019) are currently emphasising the need to reduce the workload of teachers. There is a significant drive to reduce unnecessary planning, marking and data management, and many schools have been focusing on this over the last two to three years. The Education Inspection Framework (Ofsted, 2019) addresses this aspect as part of the judgement that inspectors will make on the effectiveness of school leadership and management. However, issues relating to teacher workload are not the only factors that result in poor wellbeing. School culture significantly impacts on teachers' mental health, as do teachers' personal lives outside of school (Glazzard and Rose, 2019).

KEY RESEARCH

The problem of teacher stress is pervasive. It is evident across all sectors of education and across countries (Gray et al., 2017), and results in burnout and lower job satisfaction. However, teacher stress is not just influenced by high workloads. Research suggests that a negative school climate can lead to high rates of teacher absenteeism and staff turnover (Grayson and Alvarez, 2008). Research demonstrates that teachers who demonstrate 'presenteeism' find it more difficult to manage their classrooms effectively (Jennings and Greenberg, 2009). This is when teachers continue to work despite being ill. The quality of their work is reduced, and this affects the quality of their relationships with their students (Jennings and Greenberg, 2009), student wellbeing (Harding et al., 2019) and overall teacher performance (Beck et al., 2011; Jain et al., 2013).

School culture

The culture of the school is shaped by the leadership team. School leaders have the capacity to create positive school cultures in which staff and students can thrive. Negative school cultures can lead to staff absence and teacher stress (Grayson and Alvarez, 2008), and result in some teachers experiencing a sense of isolation.

Teachers work more effectively when they are valued by colleagues and leaders and when they have agency. If teachers do not feel valued, trusted or supported, or if they are micromanaged, they can start to experience poor wellbeing (Glazzard and Rose, 2019), particularly if they feel that they are being managed out of their jobs. In addition, toxic school cultures that expose teachers to excessive and various forms of scrutiny can also have a detrimental impact on teachers' mental health. Examples of surveillance mechanisms include learning walks, lesson observations, data drops and scrutiny of students' work. These processes have turned schools into panoptic laboratories and restricted teacher agency. Teachers are accountable to a range of stakeholders, but the levels of surveillance to which some are subjected are unnecessary and serve to undermine their self-efficacy.

Personal circumstances

Glazzard and Rose (2019) found that teachers' personal circumstances also impacted on their wellbeing. When situations arose in their personal lives that they were required to address, this was often the catalyst that resulted in them experiencing poor wellbeing. Teachers are generally dedicated, hard-working professionals. However, when they experience adverse circumstances in their personal lives, their professional and personal lives can clash (Glazzard and Rose, 2019). Examples of adverse circumstances may include parental or child illness, bereavement, divorce, or separation. These circumstances necessitate a significant investment in time to resolve the issues, and often that is when teachers begin to recognise they are not coping (Glazzard and Rose, 2019). Most teachers accept that their jobs will 'eat away' into their personal time, but when that time is taken up with addressing specific situations that demand attention, teachers may start to fall behind with their core professional duties. Personal circumstances can result in teachers leaving the profession or struggling to continue in their professional roles regardless of the fact that they are not coping.

─────── CASE STUDY ───────

A primary school teacher experienced a family bereavement. She had to organise the funeral, register the death and provide ongoing personal support to family members who were also affected by the bereavement. This quickly started to affect her job. She fell behind on her planning and marking and was unable to meet deadlines that were non-negotiable. She continued to work full-time but soon recognised that her personal circumstances were having an adverse effect on her teaching. She went into lessons unprepared, and sometimes the quality of her explanations were not clear because her mind was on other matters. Eventually, she decided to speak to the head teacher. Together, they agreed to trial a reduced teaching timetable and a flexible working day was implemented to facilitate an earlier finish at the end of the day. This gave her time to attend to personal matters. This process continued for a month but eventually the teacher requested to move on to a part-time contract. She reduced her contract to 0.6 rather than 1.0, and the funding that was saved on her salary was used to deploy another teacher who worked on a 0.4 contract. These adjustments to her working life helped her to stay in teaching.

Workload

Recent data on teacher workload indicate that:

- 78 per cent of all education professionals have experienced behavioural, psychological or physical symptoms due to their work;

- workload was found to be the major aspect of their job that teachers disliked;

- work/life balance emerged as the top issue at work for 69 per cent of education professionals in 2019;

- volume of workload was the major reason given for considering leaving the profession, with 71 per cent of education professionals citing this;

- workload remained the major aspect of working in education that professionals disliked, and if changed would most improve employee wellbeing and their work/life balance.

(ESP, 2019)

─────── CASE STUDY ───────

A secondary school took steps to reduce teacher marking. The marking policy was adapted so that teachers were not required to mark every student's work at the end of lessons. Instead, the teachers 'sampled' some of the work and marked six students' work in-depth. This enabled them to identify key misconceptions. The teachers then selected one misconception and addressed this in the next lesson. There was a greater focus on teachers providing high-quality feedback to students within lessons, and this meant that students received feedback which was more immediate. They could then act on it immediately during the lesson to achieve greater progress.

Teacher resilience

Greenfield's (2015) model of teacher resilience demonstrates that teacher resilience is not just a characteristic within the individual. Although the model acknowledges that teachers who have hope, a sense of purpose and self-efficacy (belief in their own competence) are likely to be more resilient, the model acknowledges the relational nature of resilience. According to the model, teachers are more likely to have greater resilience if they have access to supportive colleagues, a supportive leadership team, and friends and family. The model also acknowledges that their resilience is affected by their ability to problem-solve situations, their willingness to engage in self-reflection and review, and their engagement with professional development opportunities. In addition, the model acknowledges that teacher resilience is influenced by the nature of the challenges which teachers experience and the broader policy context which affects education. Teachers who are more resilient are more likely to have better wellbeing than those who are not.

Teacher agency

Teacher agency is broadly understood as the capacity of the teacher to demonstrate initiative and achieve goals. According to Pantic (2015), teacher agency is influenced by a teacher's sense of purpose, their competence, the degree of autonomy they have, and their ability to mediate or overcome barriers that obstruct their sense of purpose. Teachers who have agency are often motivated to take action because they have a clear sense of purpose. Teachers with greater self-efficacy are usually in a better position to demonstrate the capacity to take initiative because they are confident in their own abilities. In addition, teachers who are viewed by leaders as competent are often empowered with the capacity to act. They are afforded greater agency than teachers who are deemed to be less competent. Teachers with greater autonomy have greater capacity to act because they can get on and do things without restrictions being applied by leaders. Finally, the ability to overcome barriers facilitates agency because this enables teachers to move forward in achieving their goals. Where agency is restricted, this can have a detrimental effect on wellbeing (Glazzard and Rose, 2019).

NEXT STEPS

Review your own workload and consider ways that you might reduce it. If you are completing work that does not directly impact on your students, then you need to reflect on whether it is necessary for you to complete the work. Reflect on the school culture. Consider:

- how staff speak to students and how colleagues speak to each other;
- the extent to which teachers can talk openly about their own weaknesses without being judged;
- the extent to which teachers can talk openly about their own mental health without being judged;
- whether there is a collaborative culture in the school;

- whether there is a culture of fear or evidence of discrimination or bullying among staff;
- what strategies the school is implementing to reduce teacher workload;
- the extent to which diversity is valued within the school, reflected in the school environment and curriculum, and within the leadership team and governing body;
- the extent to which teachers are monitored.

What have you learned?

This chapter has argued that teacher workload is not the only factor that results in poor wellbeing for teachers. School climate, personal factors and the extent to which teachers have agency are also important factors for consideration that contribute to the mental health of teachers. In addition, the resilience of individual teachers to respond to the challenges they face within their professional roles is also a factor that influences wellbeing. Teachers with high levels of personal resilience can mitigate the effects of workload, personal circumstances and toxic school cultures. However, this chapter has emphasised that resilience is not solely a personal characteristic; it is relational and influenced by a variety of contextual factors, including access to support networks.

── FURTHER READING ────────────────

Gray, C., Wilcox, G. and Nordstokke, D. (2017) Teacher mental health, school climate, inclusive education and student learning: a review. *Canadian Psychology*, 58(3): 203–10.

Thapa, A., Cohen, D., Guffey, S. and Higgins-D'Alessandro, A. (2013) A review of school climate research. *Review of Educational Research*, 83(3): 357–85.

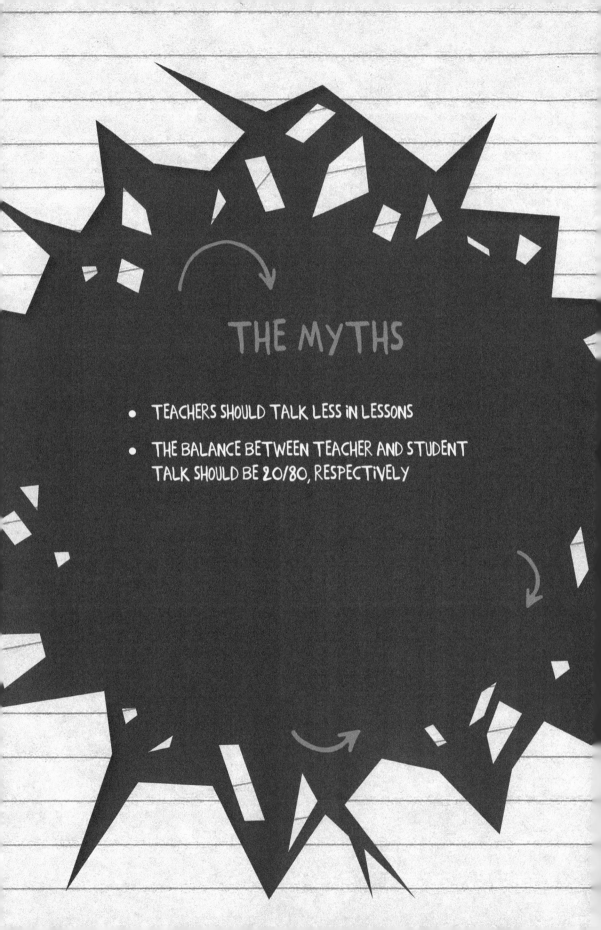

18

TEACHER TALK AND DIRECT TEACHING

What will you learn?

This chapter introduces you to key research that emphasises the importance of guided direct teaching. It highlights the importance of the use of worked examples as a pedagogical approach and examines the impact of direct instruction on the development of schema and cognitive load.

─────── WHAT ARE THE MYTHS? ───────

- Teachers should talk less in lessons.
- The balance between teacher and student talk should be 20/80, respectively.

Why should teachers challenge the myths?

For several years, myths have circulated about the amount of time that teachers should spend talking in lessons. Ofsted inspectors have commented in past inspection reports about the amount of teacher talk in lessons, and associations have been made between the amount of teacher talk and learning gains for students. The research evidence suggests that direct, guided instruction results in better learning gains for students. This form of teaching necessitates teachers to lead classroom delivery and use dialogue to alter students' thinking. If teachers do not talk in lessons, then the approach is unguided. Guided, direct, explicit teaching requires teachers to talk. The most powerful resource in the classroom is the teacher. Students require access to teacher dialogue to move through their zone of proximal development. Vygotsky (1978) argued extensively about the role of language in learning, and restricting exposure to teacher dialogue reduces opportunities for students to learn through the medium of dialogue.

KEY RESEARCH

- Moreno (2004) concluded that there is a growing body of research showing students learn more deeply from strongly guided learning.
- The worked example effect, which has been replicated a number of times, provides some of the strongest evidence for the superiority of direct teaching. Thus, students learn more when given worked examples of problems because this reduces the load on the working memory (Kirschner et al., 2006).
- Direct guidance is necessary for both effective learning and transfer (Roblyer, 1996).
- Research consistently supports direct, strong instructional guidance rather than constructivist-based minimal guidance during teaching (Kirschner et al., 2006).
- Process worksheets have been found to be effective in promoting learning (Nadolski et al., 2005). These are worksheets that include worked examples, steps through problems, and hints and tips.

The research demonstrates that students learn more through direct teacher guidance, and this approach requires teachers to use dialogue in lessons.

Guided teaching

Guided teaching refers to any form of teaching where the teacher guides student learning. This could take various forms, including whole-class delivery, group instruction, individual instruction or independent learning guided by the teacher. The research evidence cited above indicates that students learn more when they are exposed to guided forms of teaching rather than through 'discovery' approaches to learning. These approaches include problem-based learning, group project-based learning and individual research projects. However, these approaches do play an important role in learning, particularly in relation to fostering student motivation, developing metacognitive capacities, and developing autonomy and independence. Discovery learning should therefore not be discounted as an important pedagogical tool.

Guided teaching requires teachers to use dialogue, and therefore teacher talk is an essential component of effective teaching. Teachers can use dialogue to guide learning in various ways. These include:

- *Teacher explanations*: Explanations of subject content, including explanations of facts, concepts and processes.
- *Teacher modelling*: Using visual approaches combined with verbal dialogue to support students' understanding of subject content.

- *Questioning*: Using questioning to promote deeper thinking and to check students' understanding of subject content.

- *Providing feedback* to students during independent learning tasks, particularly in relation to their misconceptions, by addressing these directly with the student.

One of the myths associated with teacher talk is that it positions students as passive recipients of information. Talking at students who are passive is not an effective strategy. Effective teachers recognise that students need to be actively engaged in their learning. These teachers successfully combine teacher dialogue with tasks that students engage with during whole-class delivery. Lecturing students for a whole lesson while they sit in silence is not effective practice. This can be achieved by combining short episodes of teacher exposition with individual, group and paired tasks for students. Once these are completed, the teacher can then use dialogue to provide feedback to students. Following this, the teacher may use questioning, explanations and modelling to advance students' understanding further. Chunking the lesson in this way by moving between teacher exposition and practice tasks is an effective way of keeping students engaged and ensuring that students receive direct input from the teacher in relation to subject content. Sometimes teachers may use the bulk of the lesson for students to engage in group work or independent learning. However, the use of teacher dialogue to facilitate students' understanding during group work, paired tasks and independent learning is critical because it ensures that students develop an accurate understanding of the subject content. Teacher dialogue therefore plays a crucial role in developing students' subject-specific knowledge, understanding and skills during a variety of pedagogical approaches. It is not solely used during direct whole-class teaching.

The case studies below demonstrate how teacher dialogue can be combined with student activity to facilitate student engagement and practice.

CASE STUDY

A Year 1 teacher was teaching a mathematics lesson that focused on developing children's understanding of counting on for addition. She started by modelling the use of fingers to support addition. She demonstrated to the children how to use the fingers on both hands to calculate 3 + 2. She demonstrated that combining three fingers on one hand with two fingers on the other hand equalled five fingers in total. She then gave the children three calculations to solve using their fingers. She then modelled how to use a number line to solve calculations involving larger numbers. Using a 0–20 number line, she demonstrated how to solve 3 + 6 by starting on the larger number (6) and counting on using the smaller number (3). She explained the importance of not counting the starting number. She then gave the children an individual number line and guided them through solving three more calculations using this strategy. The teacher then modelled how to use the number line to bridge through 10. She demonstrated how to use the number line to solve 9 + 7. She then presented the class with 5 + 13 and asked them to tell her how to complete the calculation. She then repeated this with 9 + 7. She then gave the children several calculations to solve using their individual number lines and she guided them through each one. Where she spotted misconceptions developing, she stopped the children and asked specific

(Continued)

(Continued)

children to come out to the board to model the strategy. When she was sure that the children had understood and were able to use the strategy, she moved them on to an individual task in which they had to use their individual number lines to solve various calculations. She circulated around the room, identifying and addressing misconceptions, and she continued to use a combination of questioning, explanations and modelling at group and individual levels.

CASE STUDY

An English teacher demonstrated to a Year 8 class how to use evidence from the text to justify an argument. This involved modelling how to collect evidence from the text to answer a specific question about a character. The question was focused on describing the character's outward appearance. After posing the question, she asked the students to read the text and highlight important sources of evidence that would support the answer to the question. The teacher then asked the students to share their responses and these were written on the board. Questions were posed that required the students to find evidence to describe the character's personality. The teacher also asked the students to highlight one piece of evidence from the text to answer this question and then asked one student to share their response, which was written on the board. Students were given 25 minutes to write an extended character description to describe the character's personality while the teacher moved around the room and provided students with individual feedback. She addressed misconceptions through the use of questioning, explanation and modelling with individual students. At the end of the lesson, she displayed a good piece of work from a student using the visualiser, and this was analysed with the class by explaining why it was good.

Schemas

Schemas are coherent mental representations of subject content that are stored in the long-term memory. Developing accurate schemas is important to help students understand how subject-specific content is connected, but it also ensures that information can be easily retrieved from the long-term memory. Think of it as being similar to a filing cabinet or the folders of information on a computer.

Explicit guided teaching ensures that students develop accurate schemas. Constructivist theory shifts the emphasis away from teaching a subject as a body of knowledge and instead emphasises learning a subject by experiencing the processes and procedures of the subject (Handelsman et al., 2004). The emphasis on processes within unguided discovery approaches to learning means that students may not develop a comprehensive understanding of the facts, concepts and skills within the subject. It may result in vital building blocks being missed out. In addition, constructivist approaches do not pay sufficient attention to the sequencing of the subject-specific facts, concepts and skills, and this can result in students developing misconceptions, particularly in subjects that are based on linear knowledge.

Worked examples

The research evidence suggests that worked examples are particularly powerful in promoting learning gains for students. Worked examples can include:

- examples of writing;

- examples of how to complete a worksheet;

- models of the steps to follow through a problem (e.g. the steps through a mathematical problem);

- examples of finished products (e.g. in design and technology);

- examples of good answers to examination questions.

Teachers can use dialogue to explain the salient features of the worked example. This enables them to emphasise the aspects that make it effective. Teachers can also use dialogue to model a worked example. They might model the process of how to complete a mathematical calculation or how to construct a piece of writing, or they could model the process of how to conduct a scientific investigation.

Cognitive load

Through using clear explanations and effective modelling in lessons, teachers are able to reduce the cognitive load on students. Cognitive load theory suggests that discovery learning or unstructured learning may generate a heavy working memory load which is detrimental to learning. This suggestion is particularly important in the case of students who lack proper schemas to integrate the new information with their prior knowledge (Kirschner et al., 2006).

NEXT STEPS

This chapter has introduced you to the importance of teacher dialogue or teacher talk during lessons. It has presented research evidence that supports explicit guided teacher instruction which necessitates teacher dialogue. It has argued that direct instruction using teacher dialogue is critical to ensuring that students develop accurate schemas and for ensuring that students gain a comprehensive understanding of a discipline. It has argued that unguided constructivist approaches to learning play an important role in pedagogy but that they can also result in high cognitive load and the formation of incoherent schemas. When working in schools, observe how teachers teach using direct instruction. Specifically, notice how they use dialogue in their teaching to ensure that students develop accurate understanding of subject content.

What have you learned?

This chapter has highlighted the importance of direct teacher instruction. It has argued that direct teaching reduces cognitive load and leads to the accurate construction of schemas in the mind. It has emphasised that although social constructivist approaches have a place in educational pedagogy, guided and direct forms of teacher instruction produce greater gains. It has therefore illustrated that teachers should talk more in lessons rather than less.

—— FURTHER READING ——

Handelsman, J., Egert-May, D., Beichner, R., Bruns, P., Change, A., DeHaan, R., et al. (2004) Scientific teaching. *Science*, 304(5670): 521–2.

Mayer, R. (2004) Should there be a three-strikes rule against pure discovery learning? The case for guided methods of instruction. *American Psychologist*, 59(1): 14–19.

Paas, F., Renkl, A. and Sweller, J. (2004) Cognitive load theory: instructional implications of the interaction between information structures and cognitive architecture. *Instructional Science*, 32(1): 1–8.

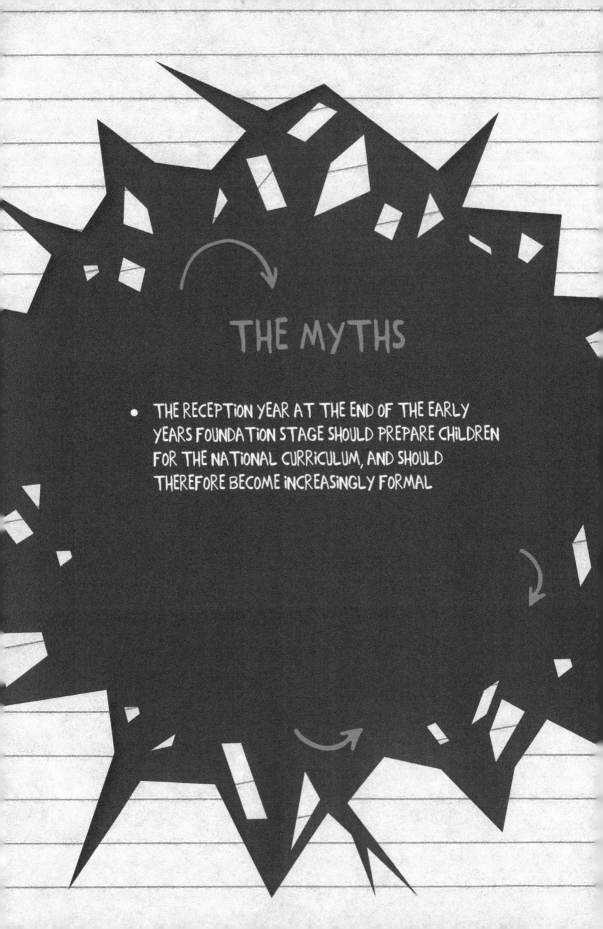

THE MYTHS

- THE RECEPTION YEAR AT THE END OF THE EARLY YEARS FOUNDATION STAGE SHOULD PREPARE CHILDREN FOR THE NATIONAL CURRICULUM, AND SHOULD THEREFORE BECOME INCREASINGLY FORMAL

19

SUPPORTING LEARNING IN THE EARLY YEARS

What will you learn?

This chapter introduces you to the key research on effective pedagogy in the early years. It emphasises the importance of play-based learning, practitioner intervention in children's play, and balancing child-initiated play with adult-directed learning. It argues that the schoolification of early years practice is potentially damaging because children may miss out on aspects of learning which are critical to securing long-term academic outcomes. Effective practice is illustrated through case studies.

WHAT ARE THE MYTHS?

- The reception year at the end of the early years foundation stage should prepare children for the national curriculum, and should therefore become increasingly formal.

Why should teachers challenge the myths?

In England in recent years, there has been an increasing prominence of a school readiness agenda and the accompanying schoolification of early years pedagogy. Policy emphasises a pedagogy that promotes school readiness in the final year of the early years foundation stage. This is associated with a more formal and restricted curriculum that does not align with the principles of effective early years pedagogy. This approach effectively restricts exposure to a broad, rich play-based curriculum in the early years that is counterproductive to long-term outcomes.

The controversial Ofsted publication *Bold Beginnings* (Ofsted, 2017) reflects the promotion of a school readiness agenda towards the end of the early years foundation stage in England. Key recommendations from this report included the following:

- make sure that the teaching of reading, including systematic synthetic phonics, is the core purpose of the reception year;

- attach greater importance to the teaching of numbers;

- ensure that when children are learning to write, resources are suitable for their stage of development and they are taught correct pencil grip and how to sit correctly at a table;

- devote sufficient time each day to the direct teaching of reading, writing and mathematics.

(Ofsted, 2017, p7)

The emphasis in this report on the teaching of mathematics and literacy skills may result in a formal curriculum in the early years by limiting children's exposure to play. In addition, it can result in communication and language and personal and physical development being marginalised, despite the fact that development in these areas is critical to securing good academic outcomes. It is essential that children in the early years are provided with learning opportunities which are developmentally appropriate. For example, children's writing skills may be impeded because they have underdeveloped motor skills. These children may require a motor skills intervention as a prerequisite to holding a pencil. Exposure to spoken language and vocabulary underpins literacy development. A stimulating, high-quality play-based curriculum will immerse children in language and support subsequent development in literacy. If children's development is rushed, the underpinning foundations may not be in place to secure positive long-term outcomes.

KEY RESEARCH

Seminal research in the early years concludes that:

- Child-initiated play, combined with the provision of teacher-initiated group work, are the most effective vehicles for learning.

- Practitioner intervention in children's freely chosen play is an effective strategy for providing intellectual challenge. Weisberg et al. (2013) refer to this strategy as 'guided play'. Guided play is neither direct teaching nor free play, but it sits between these two pedagogical approaches.

- The most effective pedagogy combines both 'teaching' and the provision of freely chosen yet potentially instructive play activities.

- The use of 'sustained shared thinking' was observed in settings where children made the most progress.

- The modelling skills or appropriate behaviour by adults were often combined with sustained periods of shared thinking in effective settings.

- Open-ended questioning and modelling were also associated with better cognitive achievement.

- Effective pedagogy for young children is less formal than for primary school.
- The most effective settings adopted discipline/behaviour policies in which staff supported children in rationalising and talking through their conflicts.

(Sylva et al., 2004)

Goswami and Bryant (2007) report evidence from neuroscience which has shown that learning depends on neural networking across visual, auditory and kinaesthetic brain regions. These findings indicate that opportunities for multisensory, active learning are critical to promoting academic and social outcomes for children in the early years.

Research also demonstrates that children who enter school with poorly developed speech and language are at high risk of literacy difficulties (Snowling et al., 2011). The focus on supporting children's communication and language development is therefore crucial in the early years, particularly for children who enter early years settings with underdeveloped skills in this domain.

The importance of developing children's social and emotional regulation skills and promoting a positive sense of self in the early years has been identified by researchers (Goodman et al., 2015). Developing these aspects supports positive longer-term outcomes (Goodman et al., 2015).

Researchers have also identified the importance of developing executive functioning skills in the early years to support long-term attainment. These include:

- *Cognitive flexibility*: Ability to switch perspectives.
- *Inhibitory control*: Ability to stay focused despite distraction, have selective focused attention, stay on task.
- *Working memory*: Ability to hold information in mind and mentally work with it; ability to remember multiple instructions in sequence and follow them in the correct order.

(Diamond, 2013)

The research suggests that a combination of play-based learning combined with teacher-directed learning is essential to support children's development. Limiting exposure to play will restrict opportunities to develop children's social and emotional regulation skills and their executive functioning skills. In addition, restricted opportunities for children to engage in play will limit opportunities for sustained shared thinking and exposure to language and vocabulary.

NEXT STEPS

This section provides more guidance on some of the evidence-based pedagogical approaches that are known to be effective in the early years.

Balancing pedagogical approaches

The research cited above suggests that children in the early years need a variety of pedagogical approaches. These include child-initiated play and adult-initiated interactions that are more typically associated with the word 'teaching'. In effective settings, the balance of who initiates the activities (i.e. children or adults) should be roughly equal (Sylva et al., 2004). Adult intervention in child-initiated play is an effective strategy that provides children with intellectual challenge. Adults can intervene in children's play to model skills, behaviour and language, or they can intervene to promote thinking through the use of high-quality open-ended questioning. Adult intervention in play can support children to operate at a higher level of development but it requires a high degree of practitioner skill. It is less effective when adults intervene and effectively close down children's play. A skilled practitioner can intervene and still allow the child to lead the play rather than imposing their own agenda on the play.

The importance of personal, social and emotional development

Personal, social and emotional development is the foundation of all learning in the early years. Children cannot learn effectively if they do not establish secure relationships with practitioners in the setting and if they do not feel safe. It is critical to invest time in establishing positive relationships with children through high-quality, caring, nurturing interactions.

Children do not necessarily arrive in the setting with good social and emotional regulation skills. A play-based pedagogy in the early years supports the development of these skills because it enables children to interact with others, and to do this effectively they need to learn how to socially interact, how to behave and how to regulate their feelings.

Social and emotional regulation

Roffey (2017) emphasises the importance of social and emotional learning in the early years. Children's social and emotional development will have been influenced by their interactions with significant others and the communities in which they live. The basic premise of social learning theory is that children will replicate the behaviour to which they have been exposed. If children have not been provided with clear boundaries in the context of the home, they may come into the early years setting thinking that specific behaviours which are tolerated in the home will also be tolerated in the preschool, nursery or school. They will quickly encounter resistance to negative behaviours, but they need to be given time to accommodate these new expectations. Their behaviours rarely alter overnight. In addition, children's social and emotional behaviours may be an attempt to communicate an unmet need. Children who experience adverse situations in their homes and communities may demonstrate a range of inappropriate behaviours, and practitioners need to be sensitive to the reasons why these behaviours may occur.

CASE STUDY

An early years setting introduced a social and emotional regulation programme. Children were taught about how to adjust their behaviour in formal and informal situations. They were taught the skills associated with being a good listener and the skills associated with being a good friend. Through stories and puppets, they were introduced to a variety of different feelings. Children were taught how to respond to the feelings of others in a sensitive way. They were also taught about the impact of their words and actions on the feelings of others. In addition, the children were taught some practical strategies to support them in managing their feelings. By the end of the intervention, they knew what to do if they felt angry, sad, frightened or frustrated. They were also introduced to both positive and negative feelings.

Sustained shared thinking

Sustained shared thinking is a process that occurs between an adult and a child. It involves skilful higher-order questioning. Within an episode, the adult takes the lead from a child and seizes an opportunity to advance the child's thinking. The research demonstrates that high-quality early years settings are characterised by frequent episodes of sustained shared thinking (Sylva et al., 2004). An example of sustained shared thinking in practice is illustrated through the case study below.

CASE STUDY

The following dialogue between a child and adult illustrates sustained shared thinking. Notice what the practitioner is doing to advance the child's learning.

A child notices that a puddle is shrinking.

Child: That puddle was massive this morning.

Adult: Why was it so big?

Child: Because it had been raining.

Adult: So, why has it got smaller?

Child: Because it has stopped raining.

Adult: Good, because it has stopped raining, the puddle won't get any bigger, but why is it drying up and shrinking?

Child: I'm not sure.

Adult: Can you think of anything else that dries up? Maybe something at home?

Child: When the clothes are wet, they dry up.

Adult: Good, where are the clothes?

Child: On the washing line.

Adult: So, what makes them go dry?

Child: The sun.

Adult: Brilliant, so why is the puddle drying up?

Child: I think the heat from the sun is drying it up.

Adult: Yes, fantastic! The heat from the sun dries the puddle and it shrinks.

Executive functioning

Executive functioning skills support children to persist with activities and to process multiple instructions at the same time. Practitioners can support the development of these skills by gradually extending the number of instructions they give to children. In addition, instructions can be presented visually so that children have a visual reminder of what they need to do next. Practitioners can intervene in children's play to model the skill of perseverance.

Talking through conflict

The research demonstrates that in less effective early years settings, children were simply told to stop inappropriate behaviour (Sylva et al., 2004). In high-quality settings, children are supported by practitioners to talk through conflict. Adults can model this initially by demonstrating the skills of effective listening and communication (e.g. use of turn-taking, eye contact and gesture). Adults can support children during these conversations to encourage them to follow simple rules (e.g. not talking over each other). Eventually, adults can withdraw and allow children to talk through the conflict and find solutions to resolve the situation.

What have you learned?

This chapter has introduced you to the key research in effective early years pedagogy. It has identified several pedagogical approaches that are effective in securing positive long-term outcomes and it has provided case studies to exemplify these.

—— FURTHER READING

Roberts-Holmes, G. (2015) The 'datafication' of early years pedagogy: 'if the teaching is good, the data should be good and if there's bad teaching, there is bad data'. *Journal of Education Policy*, 30(3): 302–15.

Whitebread, D. and Bingham, S. (2014) School readiness: starting age, cohorts and transitions in the early years. In J. Moyles, J. Georgeson and J. Payler (eds), *Early Years Foundations: Critical Issues*, 2nd edn. Berkshire: Open University Press.

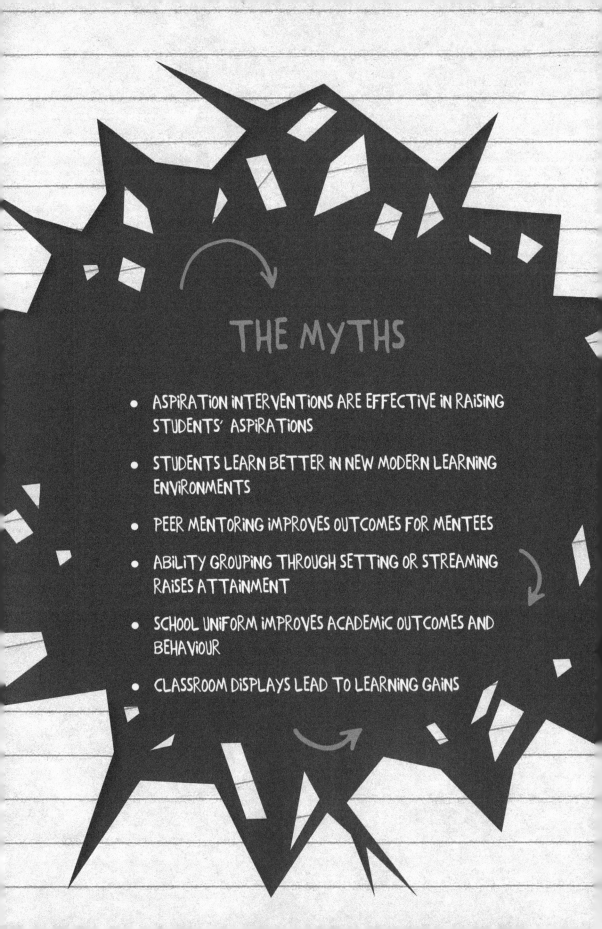

THE MYTHS

- ASPIRATION INTERVENTIONS ARE EFFECTIVE IN RAISING STUDENTS' ASPIRATIONS

- STUDENTS LEARN BETTER IN NEW MODERN LEARNING ENVIRONMENTS

- PEER MENTORING IMPROVES OUTCOMES FOR MENTEES

- ABILITY GROUPING THROUGH SETTING OR STREAMING RAISES ATTAINMENT

- SCHOOL UNIFORM IMPROVES ACADEMIC OUTCOMES AND BEHAVIOUR

- CLASSROOM DISPLAYS LEAD TO LEARNING GAINS

20

OTHER EDUCATIONAL MYTHS

What will you learn?

This chapter addresses myths that have not been considered elsewhere in this book. These are drawn from the Teaching and Learning Toolkit published by the Education Endowment Foundation (Higgins et al., 2014).

WHAT ARE THE MYTHS?

This chapter focuses on the interventions listed on the toolkit that have little or no impact on educational outcomes. These include the following assumptions:

- Aspiration interventions are effective in raising students' aspirations.
- Students learn better in new modern learning environments.
- Peer mentoring improves outcomes for mentees.
- Ability grouping through setting or streaming raises attainment.
- School uniform improves academic outcomes and behaviour.
- Classroom displays lead to learning gains.

Why should teachers challenge the myths?

Some of these interventions are extremely costly or time-consuming for schools, parents and governments. If the evidence suggests that they make little or no impact, then we need to reflect on whether they are worth the financial or time investment required.

Aspiration interventions

Evidence suggests that most students already have high aspirations. Underachievement may not therefore result from a lack of aspirations, but from a gap between what students know and can do and what they want to achieve. There is no robust evidence which suggests that aspiration interventions have consistently been successful in raising students' aspirations. There is also no robust evidence which suggests that raising aspirations results in learning gains. As a result, the EEF toolkit suggests that it may be more helpful to focus directly on raising attainment rather than raising aspirations.

CASE STUDY

A primary school developed links with the teacher training department at a local university. The lecturers and teachers planned an annual aspiration day that the teacher training students organised. This year, the children had been working on a unit of work that focused on the voyages of Christopher Columbus. The children had completed a sequence of lessons in school and the aspiration day was planned to build on this prior learning. The students worked in groups for several weeks to plan a lesson. Each group was tasked with planning and delivering a 30-minute lesson. The children rotated around each group during the day to provide them with a variety of experiences. The lessons included drama, art, science, history and geography. At the start of the day, the children went into a large lecture theatre where they were exposed to an immersive learning experience. Following this, they then participated in the lessons that the student teachers had planned. At the end of the day, they returned to the lecture theatre for a plenary and celebration event. Afterwards, several children indicated that they intended to study at the university when they were older.

Learning environment

The EEF toolkit suggests that the physical environment only results in learning gains at the extremes. For example, if students are subjected to very high noise levels, then there can be a measurable detrimental effect on learning. Extremely warm and humid conditions can cause a loss of concentration and drowsiness. Very low lighting levels can be a barrier to reading and writing, but this is not usually a problem in schools.

Mentoring

Mentoring in education involves pairing young people with an older peer or volunteer who acts as a positive role model. In general, mentoring aims to build confidence, develop resilience and character, or raise aspirations, rather than develop specific academic skills or knowledge. Mentors typically build relationships with young people by meeting with them informally to offer support or by leading activities with groups of mentees. The literature on the effectiveness of peer mentoring is generally inconclusive, but the EEF toolkit suggests that it makes little or no difference to student outcomes.

CASE STUDY

A secondary school developed the role of student mental health ambassadors. The students had to apply and be interviewed for the role. Following this, they completed a training course that addressed content including mental health, sensitive listening, confidentiality and safeguarding. The ambassadors were matched to students who needed social and emotional support. They supported these students to develop self-regulation skills and they provided them with a friendly listening ear. They provided the mentees with some strategies for managing their own mental health. Although there was no evidence of improved academic outcomes for the mentees, they enjoyed developing informal relationships with a mentor and the scheme supported their emotional wellbeing. In addition, the scheme supported the mentors to develop leadership skills. Consequently, the school considered this to be a worthwhile initiative.

Setting or streaming

The aim of setting and streaming approaches is to enable teachers to target a narrower range of pupil attainment in a class. In the UK, setting and streaming are more common in secondary school than in primary school.

- 'Setting' usually involves grouping pupils in a given year group into classes for specific subjects, such as mathematics and English, but not across the whole curriculum.

- 'Streaming' (also known as 'tracking' in some countries) usually involves grouping pupils into classes for all or most of their lessons so that a pupil is in the same group regardless of the subject being taught.

The evidence cited in the EEF toolkit suggests that setting or streaming can have a negative impact on students who are placed in lower-ability groups and that the positive impact for the higher-attaining students is very low.

School uniform

There is a general belief in many countries that school uniform supports the development of a positive whole-school ethos, and therefore supports discipline and motivation. This assumption is not supported by research evidence.

Classroom displays

The ability to focus and sustain attention on important information is essential for learning in the classroom and is positively associated with academic achievement (Erickson et al., 2015; McKinney et al., 1975; Oakes et al., 2002). Attention is the gateway to learning (Steele et al., 2012), and the more focused children are on a task, the better the learning outcome. As children get older, they sustain greater attention and even manage to stay focused when there are distractions (Gaspelin et al., 2015; Matusz et al., 2015), although their ability to focus varies between children of the same age.

Fisher et al. (2014) provided the first systematic exploration of the impact of visual displays on behaviour and learning in young children (mean age 5.5 years). They systematically manipulated the amount of visual information that children were exposed to in a lab classroom over six science lessons. Half of the lessons were delivered in a visually stimulating classroom and half were taught with no visual displays. Children visited the classroom for the six lessons over a two-week period and completed an assessment task at the end of each lesson. They were video-recorded during the lessons and their behaviour was coded in relation to their visual engagement as either being on-task (e.g. looking at the teacher, looking at their books) or off task (e.g. looking at peers, looking at the walls). In the classroom where displays were removed, children did engage in off-task behaviour. However, in the presence of lots of visual displays, children spent more time overall engaging in off-task behaviour compared to their behaviour in the classroom with no visual stimuli. Importantly, children performed significantly worse in terms of their learning in the highly visual classroom compared to their performance when in the classroom with no displays. More time spent off-task was related to poorer learning.

Emerging evidence therefore highlights that visual features of school classrooms, specifically wall displays, have implications for attention and learning (Barrett et al., 2015; Fisher et al., 2014). These studies provide the first empirical evidence for the possible detrimental impact of visual classrooms on learning.

NEXT STEPS

Research into the effects of visual sensitivities in children with autism and consider the implications of this research for practice, particularly if you have children with autism in a mainstream classroom.

What have you learned?

In this chapter, we have introduced you to a range of educational myths that have been challenged by the EEF toolkit. We have used two case studies to illustrate that there may be some positive benefits associated with these practices. We have highlighted emerging research which demonstrates that highly decorated visual classrooms may not always facilitate good behaviour and learning gains.

 **FURTHER READING**

Adey, P. and Dillon, J. (2012) *Bad Education: Debunking Myths in Education*. Maidenhead: Open University Press.

Weston, D. and Clay, B. (2018) *Unleashing Great Teaching*. London: Routledge.

CONCLUSION

This book has introduced you to some key educational myths. It has presented some key pieces of research that challenge the myths and it has used case studies to exemplify aspects of effective practice.

In the Introduction, the book highlighted the move towards an evidence-based approach to education. The government is deeply committed to commissioning educational research that is then published to provide evidence of 'what works' within educational contexts. We have argued that this process can be reductive when the research is used to promote specific pedagogical approaches to which the government is deeply committed. Current educational policy conceptualises learning as a largely individual process rather than as a social process. There is an emphasis on subject-specific knowledge and skills and knowledge retention. Pedagogical approaches that are highlighted as best practice within policy documents demonstrate an emphasis on teacher-centred approaches to learning rather than child-centred and socially constructed approaches.

The book has highlighted that the emphasis on 'what works' through research is problematic because contexts matter. The process of learning is shaped by school, family and community contexts. 'What works' in one context may not work in a different context, and the effectiveness of specific pedagogical approaches will vary between students. Schools are not scientific laboratories, and the reliability of research evidence obtained from school contexts must therefore be questioned.

This book has also emphasised the importance of teacher professionalism. Teachers are well placed and probably the best people to decide whether specific approaches will be effective within their own contexts. It is therefore important to work from the bottom up rather than the top down. Practice-based research is research that is generated from teachers' own professional practice and the contexts in which they work. It differs from research that is produced by academics in that it is based on data that teachers draw from their own classrooms and schools.

Developing communities of teacher-researchers is not a new concept. However, within the market-driven, performance-based educational climate, it offers a democratic approach in that it provides teachers with a voice. Teachers themselves are the best people to decide 'what works' within their own unique contexts. Situating teachers as researchers provides credibility to the naturally occurring data that are generated within school and classroom contexts. As a concept, it provides teachers with a credible methodology for determining what is effective and what is not with the students that they teach.

This book has not been able to address all educational myths. The need for the profession to have access to a body of research is critical so that educational practice is based on robust evidence. However, there is no reason why that evidence base cannot come from those currently working within the profession rather than from professional researchers who may not work in schools.

REFERENCES

Abbey, D.S., Hunt, D.E. and Weiser, J.C. (1985) Variations on a theme by Kolb: a new perspective for understanding counseling and supervision. *The Counseling Psychologist*, 13(3): 477–501.

Abiola, O.O. and Dhindsa, H.S. (2012) Improving classroom practices using our knowledge of how the brain works. *International Journal of Environmental and Science Education*, 7(1): 71–81.

Alexander, R., Rose, J. and Woodhead, C. (1992) *Curriculum Organisation and Classroom Practice in Primary Schools*. London: Department of Education and Science.

Allan, J. (2008) *Rethinking Inclusive Education: The Philosophers of Difference in Practice*. Dordrecht: Springer.

Allen, R. and Thompson, D. (2016) *Changing the Subject: How Are the EBacc and Attainment 8 Reforms Changing Results?* London: The Sutton Trust.

Almeida, P. (2010) Questioning patterns, questioning profiles and teaching strategies in secondary education. *International Journal of Learning*, 17(1): 587–600.

Aronson, J., Fried, C.B. and Good, C. (2001) Reducing the effects of stereotype threat on African American college students by shaping implicit theories of intelligence. *Journal of Intervention Social Psychology*, 38(2): 1–13.

Barenberg, J., Roeder, U.R. and Dutke, S. (2018) Students' temporal distributing of learning activities in psychology courses: factors of influence and effects on the metacognitive learning outcome. *Psychology Learning and Teaching*, 17(3): 257–71.

Barnes, J. and Scoffham, S. (2017) The humanities in English primary schools: struggling to survive. *Education*, 45(3): 3–13.

Barrett, P., Davies, F., Zhang, Y. and Barrett, L. (2015) The impact of classroom design on pupils' learning: final results of a holistic, multilevel analysis. *Building and Environment*, 89: 118–33.

Barron, B. and Darling-Hammond, L. (2008) How can we teach for meaningful learning? In L. Darling-Hammond, B. Barron, P.D. Pearson, A.H. Schoenfeld, E.K. Stage, T.D. Zimmerman, et al. (eds), *Powerful Learning: What We Know about Teaching for Understanding*. San Francisco, CA: Jossey-Bass.

Baumert, J., Kunter, M., Blum, W., Brunner, M., Voss, T., Jordan, A., et al. (2010) Teachers' mathematical knowledge, cognitive activation in the classroom, and student progress. *American Educational Research Journal*, 47(1): 133–80.

Beck, A., Crain, A.L., Solberg, L.I., Unützer, J., Glasgow, R.E., Maciosek, M.V., et al. (2011) Severity of depression and magnitude of productivity loss. *Annals of Family Medicine*, 9(4): 305–11.

Belland, B.R., Walker, A.E., Kim, N.J. and Lefler, M. (2016) Synthesizing results from empirical research on computer-based scaffolding in STEM education: a meta-analysis. *Review of Educational Research*, 87(2): 309–44.

Bergsteiner, H., Avery, G.C. and Neumann, R. (2010) Kolb's experiential learning model: critique from a modelling perspective. *Studies in Continuing Education*, 32(1): 29–46.

Berliner, D. (2011) Rational responses to high stakes testing: the case of curriculum narrowing and the harm that follows. *Cambridge Journal of Education*, 41(3): 287–302.

Biesta, G. (2009) Good education in an age of measurement: on the need to reconnect with the question of purpose in education. *Educational Assessment, Evaluation and Accountability*, 21(1): 33–46.

Binet, A. and Simon, T. (1916) *The Development of Intelligence in Children*. Baltimore, MD: Williams & Wilkins Co.

Bjork, E.L. and Bjork, R.A. (2011) Making things hard on yourself, but in a good way: creating desirable difficulties to enhance learning. In M.A. Gernsbacher, R.W. Pew, L.M. Hough and J.R. Pomerantz (eds), *Psychology and the Real World: Essays Illustrating Fundamental Contributions to Society*. New York: Worth Publishers.

Black, P.J. and Wiliam, D. (1998) *Inside the Black Box: Raising Standards through Classroom Attainment*. London: King's College London.

Blackwell, L., Trzesniewski, K.H. and Dweck, C.S. (2007) Implicit theories of intelligence predict achievement across an adolescent transition: a longitudinal study and an intervention. *Child Development*, 78(1): 246–63.

Blatchford, P., Russell, A. and Webster, R. (2012) *Reassessing the Impact of Teaching Assistants: How Research Challenges Practice and Policy*. London: Routledge.

Boaler, J. (2002) Learning from teaching: exploring the relationship between reform curriculum and equity. *Journal for Research in Mathematics Education*, 33(4): 239–58.

Boaler, J. (2013) Ability and mathematics: the mindset revolution that is reshaping education. *Forum*, 55(1): 143–52.

Boaler, J. (2015) *Mathematical Mindsets: Unleashing Students' Potential through Creative Math, Inspiring Messages and Innovative Teaching*. Chappaqua, NY: Jossey-Bass/Wiley.

Bolger, K.E. and Patterson, C.J. (2001) Pathways from child maltreatment to internalizing problems: perceptions of control as mediators and moderators. *Development and Psychopathology*, 13(4): 913–40.

Bor, W., Dean, A.J., Najman, J. and Hayatbakhsh, R. (2014) Are child and adolescent mental health problems increasing in the 21st century? A systematic review. *Australian and New Zealand Journal of Psychiatry*, 48(7): 606–16.

Bourdieu, P. (1986) The forms of capital. In J.E. Richardson (ed.), *Handbook of Theory and Research for the Sociology of Education*. New York: Greenword.

Brand, C. (1996) *The G Factor: General Intelligence and Its Implications*. New York: John Wiley.

Bransford, J.D., Brown, A. L., Cocking, R.R., Donovan, M.S. and Pellegrino, J.W. (2004) *How People Learn*. Washington, DC: National Academy Press.

Brighton, C.M., Hertberg, H.L., Moon, T.R., Tomlinson, C.A. and Callahan, C.M. (2005) *The Feasibility of High-End Learning in a Diverse Middle School*. Available at: http://files.eric.ed.gov/fulltext/ED505377.pdf

Britt, M. (2014) How to better engage online students with online strategies. *College Student Journal*, 49(3): 399–406.

Butkowsky, I.S. and Willows, D.M. (1980) Cognitive-motivational characteristics of children varying in reading ability: evidence for learned helplessness in poor readers. *Journal of Educational Psychology*, 72(3): 408–22.

Cantor, P., Osher, D., Berg, J., Steyer, L. and Rose, T. (2019) Malleability, plasticity, and individuality: how children learn and develop in context. *Applied Developmental Science*, 23(4): 307–37.

Cheung, A.C. and Slavin, R.E. (2013) The effectiveness of educational technology applications for enhancing mathematics achievement in K-12 classrooms: a meta-analysis. *Educational Research Review*, 9: 88–113.

Claro, S., Paunesku, D. and Dweck, C.S. (2016) Growth mindset tempers the effects of poverty on academic achievement. *Proceedings of the National Academy of Sciences USA*, 113: 8664–8.

Clausson, E. and Berg, A. (2008) Family intervention sessions: one useful way to improve school children's mental health. *Journal of Family Nursing*, 14(3): 289–312.

Coe, R., Aloisi, C., Higgins, S. and Major, L. (2014) *What Makes Great Teaching? Review of the Underpinning Research*. Available at: www.suttontrust.com/wp-content/uploads/2019/12/What-makes-great-teaching-FINAL-4.11.14-1.pdf

Coffield, F. (2012) Learning styles: unreliable, invalid and impractical and yet still widely used. In P. Adey and J. Dillon (eds), *Bad Education: Debunking Myths in Education*. Maidenhead: Open University Press.

Coffield, F., Moseley, D.V., Hall, E. and Ecclestone, K. (2004a) *Should We Be Using Learning Styles? What Research Has to Say to Practice*. London: Learning and Skills Research Centre/University of Newcastle upon Tyne.

Coffield, F., Moseley, D.V., Hall, E. and Ecclestone, K. (2004b) *Learning Styles and Pedagogy in Post-16 Learning: A Systematic and Critical Review*. London: Learning and Skills Research Centre/University of Newcastle upon Tyne.

Coopersmith, S. (1967) *The Antecedents of Self-Esteem*. San Francisco, CA: W.H. Freeman & Co.

Corrigan, P. and Watson, A. (2007) How children stigmatize people with mental illness. *International Journal of Social Psychiatry*, 53(6): 526–46.

Covington, M. (1992) *Making the Grade: A Self-Worth Perspective on Motivation and School Reform*. Cambridge: Cambridge University Press.

Creemers, B.P.M. and Kyriakides, L. (2006) Critical analysis of the current approaches to modelling educational effectiveness: the importance of establishing a dynamic model. *School Effectiveness and School Improvement*, 17(3): 347–66.

Cushman, P., Clelland, T. and Hornby, G. (2011) Health-promoting schools and mental health issues: a survey of New Zealand schools. *Pastoral Care in Education*, 29(4): 247–60.

Danby, G. and Hamilton, P. (2016) Addressing the 'elephant in the room': the role of the primary school practitioner in supporting children's mental well-being. *Pastoral Care in Education*, 34(2): 90–103.

Darling-Hammond, L., Flook, L., Cook-Harvey, C., Barron, B. and Osher, D. (2019) Implications for educational practice of the science of learning and development. *Applied Developmental Science*, 1–44.

Davies, J., Hallam, S. and Ireson, J. (2003) Ability groupings in the primary school: issues arising from practice. *Research Papers in Education*, 18(1): 45–60.

Department for Education (DfE) (2011) *Teachers' Standards: Guidance for School Leaders, School Staff and Governing Bodies*. London: DfE.

Department for Education (DfE) (2014) *Mental Health and Behaviour in Schools: Departmental Advice for School Staff*. London: DfE.

Department for Education (DfE) (2017) *Progress in International Reading Literacy Study (PIRLS): National Report for England*. London: DfE.

Department for Education (DfE) (2018) *Ways to Reduce Workload in Your School(s): Tips and Case Studies from School Leaders, Teachers and Sector Experts*. London: DfE.

Department for Education (DfE) (2019a) *Early Career Framework*. London: DfE.

Department for Education (DfE) (2019b) *ITT Core Content Framework*. London: DfE.

Department for Education (DfE) (2019c) *National Curriculum Assessments at Key Stage 2 in England, 2019*. London: DfE.

Department for Education (DfE) and Department of Health (DoH) (2015) *Special Educational Needs and Disability Code of Practice: 0 to 25 Years Statutory Guidance for Organisations Which Work with and Support Children and Young People Who Have Special Educational Needs or Disabilities*. London: DfE/DoH.

Department for Education and Skills (DfES) (2006) *Independent Review of the Teaching of Early Reading*. Nottingham: DfES.

Diamond, A. (2013) Executive functions. *Annual Review of Psychology*, 64: 135–68.

Dickins, M. (2014) *A to Z of Inclusion in Early Childhood*. Berkshire: Open University Press.

Dixon, A. (2002) Editorial. *Forum*, 44(1): 1.

Dixon, F.A., Yssel, N., McConnell, J.M. and Hardin, T. (2014) Differentiated instruction, professional development, and teacher efficacy. *Journal for the Education of the Gifted*, 37(2): 111–27.

Duckworth, A. (2017) *Grit: The Power of Passion and Perseverance*. New York: Vermilion.

Duckworth, A.L., Peterson, C., Matthews, M.D. and Kelly, D.R. (2007) Grit: perseverance and passion for long-term goals. *Journal of Personality and Social Psychology*, 92(6): 1087–101.

Dunne, L. (2009) Discourses of inclusion: a critique. *Power and Education*, 1(1): 42–56.

Dweck, C.S. (1999) *Self-Theories: Their Role in Motivation, Personality, and Development*. Hove: Psychology Press.

Dweck, C.S. (2007) Boosting achievement with messages that motivate. *Education Canada*, 47(2): 6–10.

Dweck, C.S. (2009) Mindsets: developing talent through a growth mindset. *Olympic Coach*, 21(1): 4–7.

Dweck, C.S. (2010) Even geniuses work hard. *Educational Leadership*, 68(1): 16–20.

Dweck, C.S. (2017) *Mindset*, 2nd edn. New York: Brown, Little Book Group.

Dyson, A. (2001) Special needs education as the way to equity: an alternative approach? *Support for Learning*, 16(3): 99–104.

Dyssegaard, C.B. and Larsen, M.S. (2013) *Evidence on Inclusion*. Copenhagen: Danish Clearinghouse for Educational Research.

Education Support Partnership (ESP) (2019) *Teacher Wellbeing Index 2019*. London: ESP.

Ekornes, S., Hauge, T.E. and Lund, I. (2012) Teachers as mental health promoters: a study of teachers' understanding of the concept of mental health. *International Journal of Mental Health Promotion*, 14(7): 289–310.

Elliott, V., Baird, J., Hopfenbeck, T.N., Ingram, J., Thompson, I., Usher, N., et al. (2016) *A Marked Improvement? A Review of the Evidence on Written Marking*. London: EEF.

Ellis, S. and Moss, G. (2014) Ethics, education policy and research: the phonics question reconsidered. *British Educational Research Journal*, 40(2): 241–60.

Ellis, S. and Tod, J. (2018) *Behaviour for Learning: Promoting Positive Relationships in the Classroom*. London: Routledge.

Erickson, L.C., Thiessen, E.D., Godwin, K.E., Dickerson, J.P. and Fisher, A.V. (2015) Endogenously and exogenously driven selective sustained attention: contributions to learning in kindergarten children. *Journal of Experimental Child Psychology*, 138: 126–34.

Eskin, M. (2012) The role of childhood sexual abuse, childhood gender nonconformity, self-esteem and parental attachment in predicting suicide ideation and attempts in Turkish young adults. *Suicidology Online*, 3: 114–23.

Evans, C. and Waring, M. (2011) How can an understanding of cognitive style enable trainee teachers to have a better understanding of differentiation in the classroom? *Educational Research for Policy and Practice*, 10(3): 149–69.

Farrington, C.A., Roderick, M., Allensworth, E., Nagaoka, J., Keyes, T.S., Johnson, D.W., et al. (2012) *Teaching Adolescents to Become Learners. The Role of Noncognitive Factors in Shaping School Performance: A Critical Literature Review*. Chicago, IL: University of Chicago Consortium on Chicago School Research.

Felmlee, D. and Eder, D. (1983) Contextual effects in the classroom: the impact of ability groups on student attainment. *Sociology of Education*, 56: 77–87.

Fisher, A.V., Godwin, K.E. and Seltman, H. (2014) Visual environment, attention allocation, and learning in young children: when too much of a good thing may be bad. *Psychological Science*, 25(7): 1362–70.

Francis, B., Archer, L., Hodgen, J., Pepper, D., Taylor, B. and Travers, M. (2017) Exploring the relative lack of impact of research on 'ability grouping' in England: a discourse analytic account. *Cambridge Journal of Education*, 47(1): 1–17.

Gardner, H. (1975) *The Shattered Mind*. New York: Knopf.

Gardner, H. (1982) *Art, Mind and Brain*. New York: Basic Books.

Gardner, H. (1983) *Frames of Mind: The Theory of Multiple Intelligences*. New York: Basic Books.

Gardner, H. (1999) *Intelligence Reframed*. New York: Basic Books.

Gardner, H. and Hatch, T. (1989) Multiple intelligences go to school: educational implications of the theory of multiple intelligences. *Educational Researcher*, 18(8): 4–9.

Gardner, H. and Wolf, D. (1983) Waves and streams of symbolisation. In D.R. Rogers and J.A. Sloboda (eds), *The Acquisition of Symbolic Skills*. London: Plenum.

Gardner, H., Howard, V. and Perkins, D. (1974) Symbol systems: a philosophical, psychological and educational investigation. In D. Olson (ed.), *Media and Symbols*. Chicago, IL: University of Chicago Press.

Garner, I. (2000) Problems and inconsistencies with Kolb's learning styles. *Educational Psychology*, 20(3): 341–8.

Gaspelin, N., Margett-Jordan, T. and Ruthruff, E. (2015) Susceptible to distraction: children lack top-down control over spatial attention capture. *Psychonomic Bulletin & Review*, 22(2): 461–8.

Geake, J. (2008) Neuromythologies in education. *Educational Research*, 50(2): 123–33.

Georghiades, P. (2004) From the general to the situated: three decades of metacognition. *International Journal of Science Education*, 26(3): 365–83.

Giangreco, M.F. (2010) One-to-one paraprofessionals for students with disabilities in inclusive classrooms: is conventional wisdom wrong? *Intellectual and Developmental Disabilities*, 48(1): 1–13.

Glazzard, J. (2013) A critical interrogation of the contemporary discourses associated with inclusive education in England. *Journal of Research in Special Education Needs*, 13(3): 182–8.

Glazzard, J. (2017) Assessing reading development through systematic synthetic phonics. *English in Education*, 51(1): 44–57.

Glazzard, J. (2019) A whole school approach to supporting children and young people's mental health. *Journal of Public Mental Health*, 18(4): 256–65.

Glazzard, J. and Rose, A. (2019) *The Impact of Teacher Wellbeing and Mental Health on Pupil Progress in Primary Schools*. Available at: www.leedsbeckett.ac.uk/-/media/files/schools/school-of-education/teacher-wellbeing--pupil-progress-research.pdf?la=en

Goodman, A., Joshi, H., Nasim, B. and Tyler, C. (2015) *Social and Emotional Skills in Childhood and Their Long-Term Effects on Adult Life: A Review for the Early Intervention Foundation*. London: Institute of Education/UCL.

Goswami, U. (2005) Synthetic phonics and learning to read: a cross-language perspective. *Educational Psychology in Practice*, 21(4): 273–82.

Goswami, U. and Bryant, P. (2007) *Children's Cognitive Development and Learning (Primary Review Research Survey 2/1a)*. Cambridge: University of Cambridge Faculty of Education.

Graham, L.J. and Harwood, V. (2011) Developing capabilities for social inclusion: engaging diversity through inclusive school communities. *International Journal of Inclusive Education*, 15(1): 135–52.

Gray, C., Wilcox, G. and Nordstokke, D. (2017) Teacher mental health, school climate, inclusive education and student learning: a review. *Canadian Psychology*, 58(3): 203–10.

Grayson, J.L. and Alvarez, H.K. (2008) School climate factors relating to teacher burnout: a mediator model. *Teaching and Teacher Education*, 24(5): 1349–63.

Greenberg, M.T., Weissberg, R.P., O'Brien, M.U., Zins, J.E., Fredericks, L., Resnik, H., et al. (2003) Enhancing school-based prevention and youth development through coordinated social, emotional, and academic learning. *American Psychologist*, 58(6–7): 466–74.

Greenfield, B. (2015) How can teacher resilience be protected and promoted? *Educational and Child Psychology*, 32(4): 52–69.

Gumora, G. and Arsenio, W.F. (2002) Emotionality, emotion regulation, and school performance in middle school children. *Journal of School Psychology*, 40(5): 395–413.

Haelermans, C., Ghysels, J. and Prince, F. (2015) Increasing performance by differentiated teaching? Experimental evidence of the student benefits of digital differentiation. *British Journal of Educational Technology*, 46(6): 1161–74.

Handelsman, J., Egert-May, D., Beichner, R., Bruns, P., Change, A., DeHaan, R., et al. (2004) Scientific teaching. *Science*, 304(5670): 521–2.

Harding, S., Morris, R., Gunnell, D., Ford, T., Hollingworth, W., Tilling, K., et al. (2019) Is teachers' mental health and wellbeing associated with students' mental health and wellbeing? *Journal of Affective Disorders*, 242: 180–7.

Hart, S., Dixon, A., Drummond, M.J. and McIntyre, D. (2004) *Learning without Limits*. Maidenhead: Open University Press.

Hattie J. and Timperley, H. (2007) The power of feedback. *Review of Educational Research*, 77(1): 81–112.

Hayes, A.M. and Bulat, J. (2017) *Disabilities Inclusive Education Systems and Policies Guide for Low- and Middle-Income Countries: Occasional Paper*. Research Triangle Park, NC: RTI Press.

Hehir, T., Gridal, T., Freeman, B., Lamoreau, R., Borquaye, Y. and Burke, S. (2016) *A Summary of the Evidence on Inclusive Education*. Sao Paulo: Instituto Alana.

Hertberg-Davis, H. (2009) Myth 7: differentiation in the regular classroom is equivalent to gifted programs and is sufficient – classroom teachers have the time, the skill, and the will to differentiate adequately. *Gifted Child Quarterly*, 53(4): 251–3.

Higgins, S., Katsipataki, M., Kokotsaki, D., Coleman, R., Major, L.E. and Coe, R. (2014) *The Sutton Trust/ Education Endowment Foundation Teaching and Learning Toolkit*. London: EEF. Available at: https://educationendowmentfoundation.org.uk/evidence-summaries/teaching-learning-toolkit

Honey, P. and Mumford, A. (2000) *The Learning Styles Helper's Guide*. Maidenhead: Peter Honey Publications.

Howard-Jones, P.A. (2014) Evolutionary perspectives on mind, brain and education. *Mind, Brain, and Education*, 8(1): 21–33.

Ireson, J. (1999) *Innovative Grouping Practices in Secondary Schools: Research Report No 166*. Available at: http://dera.ioe.ac.uk/4460/1/RR166.pdf

Ivie, S. (2009) Learning styles: Humpty Dumpty revisited. *Érudit*, 44(2): 177–92.

Jain, G., Roy, A., Harikrishnan, V., Yu, S., Dabbous, O. and Lawrence, C. (2013) Patient-reported depression severity measured by the PHQ-9 and impact on work productivity: results from a survey of full-time employees in the United States. *Journal of Occupational and Environmental Medicine*, 55(3): 252–8.

Jennings, P.A. and Greenberg, M.T. (2009) The prosocial classroom: teacher social and emotional competence in relation to student and classroom outcomes. *Review of Educational Research*, 79(1): 491–525.

Jindal-Snape, D. and Miller, D.J. (2010) Understanding transitions through self-esteem and resilience. In D. Jindal-Snape (ed.), *Educational Transitions*. London: Routledge.

Johnson, D.W., Johnson, R.T. and Stanne, M.E. (2000) *Cooperative Learning Methods: A Meta-Analysis*. Available at: www.researchgate.net/publication/220040324_Cooperative_learning_methods_A_meta-analysis

Johnston, R. and Watson, J. (2007) *Teaching Synthetic Phonics*. Exeter: Learning Matters.

Kirschner, P.A., Sweller, J. and Clark, R.E. (2006) Why minimal guidance during instruction does not work: an analysis of the failure of constructivist, discovery, problem-based, experiential, and inquiry-based teaching. *Educational Psychologist*, 41(2): 75–86.

Klein, P.D. (1997) Multiplying the problems of intelligence by eight: a critique of Gardner's theory. *Canadian Journal of Education*, 22(4): 377–94.

Kolb, D.A. (1984) *Experiential Learning: Experience as the Source of Learning and Development*. Englewood Cliffs, NJ: Prentice Hall.

Konstantinou-Katzi, P., Tsolaki, E., Meletiou-Mavrotheris, M. and Koutselini, M. (2013) Differentiation of teaching and learning mathematics: an action research study in tertiary education. *International Journal of Mathematical Education in Science and Technology*, 44(3): 332–49.

Kruzich, J.M., Friesen, B.J. and Van Soest, D. (1986) Assessment of student and faculty learning styles: research and application. *Journal of Social Work Education*, 3: 22–30.

Landerl, K. (2000) Influences of orthographic consistency and reading instruction on the development of nonword reading skills. *European Journal of Psychology of Education*, 15: 239–57.

Lee, E. and Hannafin, M.J. (2016) A design framework for enhancing engagement in student-centered learning: own it, learn it, and share it. *Educational Technology Research and Development*, 64(4): 707–34.

Maguire, E.A., Woollett, K. and Spiers, H.J. (2006) London taxi drivers and bus drivers: a structural MRI and neuropsychological analysis. *Hippocampus*, 16(12): 1091–101.

Maier, S.F. and Seligman, M.E.P. (1976) Learned helplessness: theory and evidence. *Journal of Experimental Psychology: General*, 105(1): 3–46.

Malecki, C. and Elliot, S. (2002) Children's social behaviours as predictors of academic achievement: a longitudinal analysis. *School Psychology Quarterly*, 17(1): 1–23.

Marzano, R.J., Marzano, J.S. and Pickering, D.J. (2003) *Classroom Management That Works: Research-Based Strategies for Every Teacher*. Alexandria, VA: ASCD.

Matusz, P.J., Broadbent, H., Ferrari, J., Forrest, B., Merkley, R. and Scerif, G. (2015) Multi-modal distraction: insights from children's limited attention. *Cognition*, 136: 156–65.

McKinney, J.D., Mason, J., Perkerson, K. and Clifford, M. (1975) Relationship between classroom behaviour and academic achievement. *Journal of Educational Psychology*, 67: 198–203.

Middleton, J. and Spanias, P. (1999) Motivation for achievement in mathematics: findings, generalizations, and criticisms of the research. *Journal for Research in Mathematics Education*, 30(1): 65–88.

Moore, D.S. (2015) *The Developing Genome: An Introduction to Behavioral Epigenetics*. New York: Oxford University Press.

Moreno, R. (2004) Decreasing cognitive load in novice students: effects of explanatory versus corrective feedback in discovery-based multimedia. *Instructional Science*, 32(1–2): 99–113.

Morgan, H. (1992) *An Analysis of Gardner's Theory of Multiple Intelligence*. Paper presented at the annual meeting of the Eastern Educational Research Association, ERIC document reproduction service, no. ED 360 088.

Moyles, J. and Suschitzky, W. (1997) The employment and deployment of classroom support staff: head teachers' perspectives. *Research in Education*, 58(1): 21–34.

Mruk, C. (1999) *Self-Esteem: Research, Theory and Practice*. London: Free Association Books.

Munro, J. (2012) *Effective Strategies for Implementing Differentiated Instruction*. Available at: http://research.acer.edu.au/cgi/viewcontent.cgi?article=1144&context=research_conference

Nadolski, R.J., Kirschner, P.A. and van Merriënboer, J.J.G. (2005) Optimising the number of steps in learning tasks for complex skills. *British Journal of Educational Psychology*, 75(2): 223–37.

Neisser, U., Boodoo, G., Bouchard, T.J., Boykin, A.W., Brody, N., Ceci, S.J., et al. (1996) Intelligence: knowns and unknowns. *American Psychologist*, 51(2): 77–101.

Nettelbeck, T. and Wilson, C. (2005) Intelligence and IQ: what teachers should know. *Educational Psychology: An International Journal of Experimental Educational Psychology*, 25(6): 609–30.

Nulty, D.D. and Barrett, M.A. (1996) Transitions in students' learning styles. *Studies in Higher Education*, 21(3): 333–45.

Oakes, L.M., Kannass, K.N. and Shaddy, D.J. (2002) Developmental changes in endogenous control of attention: the role of target familiarity on infants' distraction latency. *Child Development*, 73(6): 1644–55.

Ofsted (2002) *The Curriculum in Successful Primary Schools*. Available at: http://dera.ioe.ac.uk/4564/1/Curriculum%20in%20successful%20primary%20schools%20%28The%29%20%28PDF%20format%29.pdf

Ofsted (2017) *Bold Beginnings: The Reception Curriculum in a Sample of Good and Outstanding Primary Schools*. Manchester: Ofsted.

Ofsted (2019) *Education Inspection Framework: Overview of Research*. Manchester: Ofsted.

Ollerton, M. (2001) Inclusion, learning and teaching mathematics: beliefs and values. In P. Gates (ed.), *Issues in Mathematics Teaching*. London: RoutledgeFalmer.

Paas, F., Renkl, A. and Sweller, J. (2003) Cognitive load theory: instructional implications of the interaction between information structures and cognitive architecture. *Instructional Science*, 32(1–2): 1–8.

Palmquist, M. and Young, R. (1992) The notion of giftedness and student expectations about writing. *Written Communication*, 9(1): 137–68.

Pantic, N. (2015) A model for study of teacher agency for social justice. *Teachers and Teaching*, 21(6): 759–78.

Pashler, H., McDaniel, M., Rohrer, D. and Bjork, R. (2009) Learning styles: concepts and evidence. *Psychological Science in the Public Interest*, 9(3): 105–19.

Petty, G. (2004) *Differentiation: What and How*. Available at: http://geoffpetty.com/training-materials/differentiation/

Petty, G. (2014) *Evidence-Based Teaching: A Practical Approach*, 2nd edn. Oxford: Oxford University Press.

Piaget, J. (1952) *The Origins of Intelligence in Children*. New York: International Universities Press.

Piaget, J. (1975) *The Equilibration of Cognitive Structure*. Chicago, IL: University of Chicago Press.

Polesel, J., Rice, S. and Dulfer, N. (2014) The impact of high-stakes testing on curriculum and pedagogy: a teacher perspective from Australia. *Journal of Education Policy*, 29(5): 640–57.

Prever, M. (2006) *Mental Health in Schools*. London: SAGE.

Price, R. (2018) *Inclusive and Special Education Approaches in Developing Countries*. Available at: https://assets.publishing.service.gov.uk/media/5c6ac403ed915d4a39787401/373_Inclusive_and_Special_Education_Approaches.pdf

Price-Mohr, R.M. and Price, C.B. (2018) Synthetic phonics and decodable instructional reading texts: how far do these support poor readers? *Dyslexia*, 24(2): 190–6.

Public Health England (PHE) (2015) *Promoting Children and Young People's Emotional Health and Wellbeing*. London: PHE.

Pullmann, H. and Allik, J. (2008) Relations of academic and general self-esteem to school achievement. *Personality and Individual Differences*, 45(6): 559–64.

Radford, J., Blatchford, P. and Webster, R. (2011) Opening up and closing down: comparing teacher and TA talk in mathematics lessons. *Learning and Instruction*, 21(5): 625–35.

Raschick, M., Maypole, D.E. and Day, P.A. (1998) Improving field education through Kolb's learning theory. *Journal of Social Work Education*, 34(1): 31–42.

Rawson, A. and Kintsch, W. (2005) Rereading effects depend on time of test. *Journal of Educational Psychology*, 97(1): 70–80.

Richland, L.E., Bjork, R.A., Finley, J.R. and Linn, M.C. (2005) Linking cognitive science to education: generation and interleaving effects. In B.G. Bara, L. Barsalou and M. Bucciarelli (eds), *Proceedings of the Twenty-Seventh Annual Conference of the Cognitive Science Society*. Mahwah, NJ: Lawrence Erlbaum.

Riener, C. and Willingham, D. (2010) The myth of learning styles. *Change: The Magazine of Higher Learning*, 42(5): 32–5.

Roblyer, M.D. (1996) The constructivist/objectivist debate: implications for instructional technology research. *Learning and Leading with Technology*, 24(2): 12–16.

Roediger, H.L. and Karpicke, J.D. (2006) Test-enhanced learning: taking memory tests improves long-term retention. *Psychological Science*, 17(3): 249–55.

Roffey, S. (2017) Ordinary magic needs ordinary magicians: the power and practice of positive relationships for building youth resilience and wellbeing. *Kognition & Pædagogik*, 103: 38–57.

Rogers, C.R. (1961) *On Becoming a Person: A Therapist's View of Psychotherapy*. Boston, MA: Houghton Mifflin.

Rohrer, D., Dedrick, R. and Stershic, S. (2015) Interleaved practice improves mathematics learning. *Journal of Educational Psychology*, 107(3): 900–8.

Rosenshine, B. (2010) *Principles of Instruction*. Available at: www.ibe.unesco.org/fileadmin/user_upload/Publications/Educational_Practices/EdPractices_21.pdf

Rosenshine, B. (2012) *Principles of Instruction: Research-Based Principles That All Teachers Should Know*. Available at: www.aft.org/pdfs/americaneducator/spring2012/Rosenshine.pdf

Rubie-Davies, C., Blatchford, P., Webster, R., Koutsoubou, M. and Bassett, P. (2010) Enhancing student learning? A comparison of teacher and teaching assistant interaction with pupils. *School Effectiveness and School Improvement*, 21(4): 429–49.

Ryan, R. and Deci, E. (2000) Intrinsic and extrinsic motivations: classic definitions and new directions. *Contemporary Educational Psychology*, 25(1): 54–67.

Ryan, R. and Deci, E. (2006) Self-regulation and the problem of human autonomy: does psychology need choice, self-determination, and will? *Journal of Personality*, 74(6): 1557–86.

Scheerens, J. and Bosker, R. (1997) *The Foundations of Educational Effectiveness*. Oxford: Pergamon.

Seidel, T. and Shavelson, R.J. (2007) Teaching effectiveness research in the past decade: the role of theory and research design in disentangling meta-analysis results. *Review of Educational Research*, 77(4): 454–99.

Seymour, P.H.K., Aro, M. and Erskine, J.M. (2003) Foundation literacy acquisition in European orthographies. *British Journal of Psychology*, 94(2): 143–74.

Sharples, J., Webster, R. and Blatchford, P. (2015) *Making Best Use of Teaching Assistants: Guidance Report*. London: EEF.

Sisak, M., Varnick, P., Varnik, A., Apter, A., Balazs, J., Balint, M., et al. (2014) Teacher satisfaction with school and psychological well-being affects readiness to help children with mental health problems. *Health Education Journal*, 73(4): 382–93.

Skidmore, D. (2004) *Inclusion: The Dynamic of School Development*. Maidenhead: Open University Press.

Slavich, G.M. and Cole, S.W. (2013) The emerging field of human social genomics. *Clinical Psychological Science*, 1(3): 331–48.

Slavin, R.E. (1987) Ability grouping and student achievement in elementary schools: a best-evidence synthesis. *Review of Educational Research*, 57(3): 293–336.

Slavin, R.E. (1990) Achievement effects of ability grouping in secondary schools: a best-evidence synthesis. *Review of Educational Research*, 60(3): 471–99.

Slee, R. (2011) *The Irregular School: Exclusion, Schooling and Inclusive Education*. London: Routledge.

Snowling, M.J., Hulme, C., Bailey, A.M., Stothard, S.E. and Lindsay, G. (2011) *Better Communication Research Programme: Language and Literacy Attainment of Pupils during Early Years and through KS2 – Does Teacher Assessment at Five Provide a Valid Measure of Children's Current and Future Educational Attainments?* London: DfE.

Spencer, L.H. and Hanley, J.R. (2003) Effects of orthographic transparency on reading and phoneme awareness in children learning to read in Wales. *British Journal of Psychology*, 94(1): 1–28.

Spinath, B. and Steinmayr, R. (2012) The roles of competence beliefs and goal orientations for change in intrinsic motivation. *Journal of Educational Psychology*, 104(4): 1135–48.

Steele, A., Karmiloff-Smith, A., Cornish, K. and Scerif, G. (2012) The multiple subfunctions of attention: differential developmental gateways to literacy and numeracy. *Child Development*, 83(6): 2028–41.

Steenbergen-Hu, S., Makel, M.C. and Olszewski-Kubilius, P. (2016) What one hundred years of research says about the effects of ability grouping and acceleration on K–12 students' academic achievement. *Review of Educational Research*, 86(4): 849–99.

Sternberg, R.J. (1983) How much gall is too much gall? A review of *Frames of Mind: The Theory of Multiple Intelligences*. *Contemporary Education Review*, 2(3): 215–24.

Sternberg, R.J. (1999) *Thinking Styles*. Cambridge: Cambridge University Press.

Sternberg, R.J. (2005) Intelligence, competence, and expertise. In A. Elliot and C.S. Dweck (eds), *The Handbook of Competence and Motivation*. New York: Guilford Press.

Stringer, E., Lewin, C. and Coleman, R. (2019) *Using Digital Technology to Improve Learning: Guidance Report*. London: EEF.

Strydom, J. and Du Plessis, S. (2000) *IQ Test: Where Does It Come from and What Does it Measure?* Available at: www.audiblox2000.com/dyslexia_dyslexic/dyslexia014.htm

Stuart, M. (2006) Teaching reading: why start with systematic phonics teaching? *Psychology of Education Review*, 30(2): 6–17.

Sweller, J. (2011) Cognitive load theory. *Psychology of Learning and Motivation*, 55: 37–76.

Sylva, K., Melhuish, E., Sammons, P., Siraj-Blatchford, I. and Taggart, B. (2004) *The Effective Provision of Pre-School Education (EPPE) Project: Findings from Pre-School to End of Key Stage 1*. London: Institute of Education.

Tanaka, M., Wekerle, C., Schmuck, M.L., Paglia-Boak, A. and MAP Research Team (2011) The linkages among childhood maltreatment, adolescent mental health, and self-compassion in child welfare adolescents. *Child Abuse & Neglect*, 35(10): 887–98.

Taylor, B., Francis, B., Archer, L., Hodgen, J., Pepper, D., Tereshchenko, A., et al. (2017) Factors deterring schools from mixed attainment teaching practice. *Pedagogy, Culture, and Society*, 25(3): 327–45.

Taylor, S. (2017) Contested knowledge: a critical review of the concept of differentiation in teaching and learning. *Warwick Journal of Education: Transforming Teaching*, 1: 55–68.

Terman, L.M. (1916) *The Uses of Intelligence Tests*. Boston, MA: Houghton Mifflin.

Terman, L.M. and Oden, M.H. (1947) *The Gifted Child Grows Up: Twenty-Five Years' Follow-Up of a Superior Group*. Stanford, CA: Stanford University Press.

Terwel, J. (2005) Curriculum differentiation: multiple perspectives and developments in education. *Journal of Curriculum Studies*, 37(6): 653–70.

The Children's Society (2014) *The Good Childhood Report 2014*. London: The Children's Society.

Thomas, G. and Loxley, A. (2007) *Deconstructing Special Education and Constructing Inclusion*. Maidenhead: Open University Press.

Thurstone, L.L. (1938) *Primary Mental Abilities*. Chicago, IL: University of Chicago Press.

Tomlinson, C.A. (2000) *Differentiation of Instruction in the Elementary Grades*. Washington, DC: Office of Educational Research and Improvement.

Torgerson, C.J., Brooks, G. and Hall, J. (2006) *A Systematic Review of the Research Literature on the Use of Phonics in the Teaching of Reading and Spelling*. London: DfES.

Torrance, H. (2017) Blaming the victim: assessment, examinations, and the responsibilisation of students and teachers in neo-liberal governance. *Discourse: Studies in the Cultural Politics of Education*, 38(1): 83–96.

Vickerman, P. (2009) *Differentiation: Guidance for Inclusive Teaching*. Available at: http://webarchive. nationalarchives.gov.uk/20101021152907/http://www.ttrb.ac.uk/ViewArticle2.aspx?anchorId=17756 &selectedId=17759&menu=17834&expanded=False&ContentId=15712

Vygotsky, L.S. (1978) *Mind in Society: The Development of Higher Psychological Processes*. Cambridge, MA: Harvard University Press.

Walton, P.D., Bowden, M.E., Kurtz, S.L. and Angus, M. (2001) Evaluation of a rime-based reading program with Shuswap and Heiltsuk First Nations prereaders. *Reading and Writing*, 14(3–4): 229–64.

Waterhouse, L. (2006) Inadequate evidence for multiple intelligences, Mozart effect and emotional intelligence theories. *Educational Psychologist*, 41(4): 247–55.

Watson, J.E. and Johnston, R.S. (1998) Accelerating reading attainment: the effectiveness of synthetic phonics. *Interchange*, 57.

Wayne, A.J. and Youngs, P. (2003) Teacher characteristics and student achievement gains: a review. *Review of Educational Research*, 73(1): 89–122.

Weisberg, D.S., Hirsh-Pasek, K. and Golinkoff, R.M. (2013) Guided play: where curricular goals meet a playful pedagogy. *Mind, Brain, and Education*, 7(2): 104–12.

Werner, E.E. (2000) Protective factors and individual resilience. In J.P. Shonkoff and S.J. Meisels (eds), *Handbook of Early Childhood Intervention*. Cambridge: Cambridge University Press.

White, J. (2005) *The Myth of Howard Gardner's Multiple Intelligences*. London: Institute of Education.

White, J. (2006) *Intelligence, Destiny and Education: The Ideological Roots of Intelligence Testing*. London: Routledge.

White, R. (1963) Ego and reality in psychoanalytic theory: a proposal regarding independent ego energies. *Psychological Issues*, 3: 125–50.

Wolke, D., Copeland, W., Angold, A. and Costello, J. (2013) Impact of bullying in childhood on adult health, wealth, crime and social outcomes. *Psychological Science*, 24(10): 1958–70.

Wyse, D. and Goswami, U. (2008) Synthetic phonics and the teaching of reading. *British Educational Research Journal*, 34(6): 691–710.

Wyse, D. and Styles, M. (2007) Synthetic phonics and the teaching of reading: the debate surrounding England's 'Rose Report'. *Literacy*, 41(1): 35–42.

Young, M. (2013) Overcoming the crisis in curriculum theory: a knowledge-based approach. *Journal of Curriculum Studies*, 45(2): 101–18.

Zins, J.E., Weissberg, R.P., Wang, M.L. and Walberg, H.J. (eds) (2004) *Building School Success through Social and Emotional Learning: Implications for Practice and Research*. New York: Teachers College Press.

iNDEX

Note: References in *italics* are to figures, those in **bold** to tables.